European Distance and E-Learning Network Online Research Workshop 2020

Enhancing the Human Experience of Learning with Technology - New Challenges for Research into Digital, Open, Distance & Networked Education

Held Online due to COVID-19

Lisbon, Portugal
21 – 23 October 2020

Editors:

Sandra Kucina Softic
Antonio Teixeira
Andras Szucs

ISBN: 978-1-7138-2385-8

Printed from e-media with permission by:

Curran Associates, Inc.
57 Morehouse Lane
Red Hook, NY 12571

CURRAN ASSOCIATES INC. proceedings.com

Some format issues inherent in the e-media version may also appear in this print version.

European Distance and E-Learning Network (EDEN)
Budapest University of Technology & Economics
H-1111 Budapest, Egry J. u.1.
Hungary

secretariat@eden-online.org

Additional copies of this publication are available from:

Curran Associates, Inc.
57 Morehouse Lane
Red Hook, NY 12571 USA
Phone: 845-758-0400
Fax: 845-758-2633
Email: curran@proceedings.com
Web: www.proceedings.com

SHORT PAPER BOOK
European Distance and E-Learning Network (EDEN)

Enhancing the Human Experience of Learning with Technology

New challenges for research into digital, open, distance & networked education

EDEN 2020 Online Research Workshop

hosted by

Universidade Aberta, Portugal

21-23 October 2020

Edited by

Sandra Kucina Softic, Antonio Teixeira, Andras Szucs
on behalf of the European Distance and E-Learning Network

Enhancing the Human Experience of Learning with Technology
Short Paper Book
2020 Research Workshop | Lisbon, 21-23 October, 2020

Published by the European Distance and E-Learning Network

Editors:
Sandra Kucina Softic
Antonio Teixeira
Andras Szucs

Editorial co-ordination:
Judit Komuves
Gabor Roman

EDEN Secretariat, c/o Budapest University of Technology and Economics
H-1111 Budapest, Egry J. u. 1, Hungary
Tel: (36) 1 463 1628, 463 2537
E-mail: secretariat@eden-online.org
http://www.eden-online.org

Supported by the Erasmus+ Programme of the European Union
The publication reflects the authors' view, the EACEA and the European Commission are not responsible for any use that may be made of the information it contains.

Introduction

The theme and scope of EDEN's RW11 intends to reflect the current challenges researchers face regarding the impact of the emerging digital technologies and Artificial Intelligence in the improvement of the quality and the sustainability of the human learning experience. The capability of generating, processing and managing more data and information than ever before during the teaching and learning process allows teachers as well as learners to be more in control. They can make better and more on the spot decisions on more elaborate and valid information, track learning performance more accurately and thoroughly, anticipate problems more astutely and act accordingly, collect more learning evidence, as well as assess and credit more transparently. In short, they can shape together their teaching and learning experiences more efficiently and collaboratively.

By upscaling and accelerating the adoption of distance and online education across the world, the Covid-19 pandemic has demonstrated the importance of rethinking the educational process as an integral part of authentic digital life experience for its main actors. In this massive collective experience of change, the role of the educational institutions, teachers, learners, their families and communities is rapidly transforming. As a result, new challenges for researchers have emerged that need to be addressed. How to assure truly equitable and socially fair access to digital learning opportunities? How to conduct effective online learning in non-adult populations? How to improve teachers' and learners' digital competences for teaching and learning? How may AI and machine learning contribute to enhancing the education process and making it more flexible and personal? How can we conduct more authentic and reliable digital assessment?

On the other hand, what are the ethical implications of the use of these digital technologies? How should learning processes be designed to contribute to the learners' well-being and mental health? How should quality of online learning provision be assured? These and many other questions have been emerging within the specialised research community. A community which is itself experiencing a process of expansion due to the growing interest in the field.

Andras Szucs
EDEN Secretary General

Antonio Moreira Teixeira
Universidade Aberta, Lisbon

Sandra Kucina Softic
EDEN President

Acknowledgement and thanks are given to the Programme and Evaluation Committee

Sandra Kucina Softic, EDEN President, University of Zagreb, Croatia
Antonio Moreira Teixeira, LE@D, Universidade Aberta, Portugal

Josep Maria Duart, Open University of Catalonia (UOC), Spain
Diana Andone, Politehnica University of Timisoara, Romania
Ulrich Bernath, Ulrich Bernath Foundation for Research in ODL, Germany
Alan Tait, The Open University, United Kingdom
Inés Gil Jaurena, National University of Distance Education (UNED), Spain
Lina Morgado, Scientific coordinator of LE@D, Universidade Aberta, Portugal
Lisa Marie Blaschke, Carl von Ossietzky University of Oldenburg, Germany
Mark Brown, National Institute for Digital Learning, Dublin City University, Ireland
Elena Caldirola, University of Pavia, Italy
Helga Dorner, Central European University, Hungary
Josep Maria Duart, Open University of Catalonia (UOC), Spain
Ulf-Daniel Ehlers, Co-Operative State University Baden-Wurttemberg (DHBW), Germany
Rebecca Galley, The Open University, United Kingdom
Vlad Mihaescu, Politehnica University of Timisoara, Romania
Don Olcott Jr., Global Higher Education Consultant, Romania
Ebba Ossiannilsson, Swedish Association of Distance Education, Sweden
Wim Van Petegem, Katholieke Universiteit Leuven, Belgium
Antonella Poce, University Roma III, Italy
Timothy Read, National University of Distance Education (UNED), Spain
Alfredo Soeiro, University of Porto, Portugal
Andras Szucs, EDEN, United Kingdom
Ferenc Tatrai, EDEN, United Kingdom
Luisa Aires, LE@D, Universidade Aberta, Portugal
Lucia Amante, LE@D, Universidade Aberta, Portugal
Antonio Quintas, LE@D, Universidade Aberta, Portugal
Alda Pereira, LE@D, Universidade Aberta, Portugal
José Bidarra, LE@D, Universidade Aberta, Portugal
Maria do Carmo Teixeira Pinto, LE@D, Universidade Aberta, Portugal
Teresa Cardoso, LE@D, Universidade Aberta, Portugal
José Mota, LE@D, Universidade Aberta, Portugal
Sandra Caeiro, LE@D, Universidade Aberta, Portugal
Isolina Oliveira, LE@D, Universidade Aberta, Portugal

TABLE OF CONTENTS

INTEGRATING THE LEARNING BY DESIGN PEDAGOGY IN TEACHER TRAINING – FUTURE DEVELOPMENT OF LEARNING PROCESSES IN AN ONLINE ENVIRONMENT WITH EDUCATIONAL DATA MINING

Jonas Bäckelin, Linköping University, Sweden

Abstract

A professional teacher continuously observes and reflect on their teaching practice related to the intended learning outcomes (ILOs). Assessment for learning (AFL) is an approach to learning processes that rely on feedback to improve students' performance and allow for embedded assessment. The general idea is that students need to know what skills, knowledge or understanding they are expected to learn in order to improve their performance (i.e. learning intentions). They also need to understand how they will be assessed, so that they can evaluate whether they have learned what was expected (i.e. success criteria and rubrics). It is also important that students learn how to self-assess to monitor their own learning, which can be facilitated by teachers using constructive alignment (i.e. self-directed learning). It is also a common strategy to train students to provide effective feedback to their peers, since this process benefits both the student who gives the feedback and the student who receives it (i.e. peer feedback). The main focus for this study is on how assessment activities designed to produce an evaluation of student performance also can be used in formative ways (i.e. educational data mining).

The bold statement is that online learning processes allows us to replace traditional assessment with learning analytics collected from machine assessment, embedded data, and incidental data. The research of Bill Cope and Mary Kalantzis (2016) has managed to apply artificial intelligence and big data analytics to e-learning ecologies. This changes the role of the educator, from transmitter of content to passive learners, to designer of a learning ecology.

Keywords: Assessment for Learning, Embedded assessment, Educational Data Mining, Learning-by-Design pedagogy, Self-directed learning

Introduction

This a study in progress is the final requirement for the international Master program Adult Learning and Global Change (ALGC), offered by the University of Linköping in collaboration with the Canadian University of British Columbia, the South African University of Western Cape and the Australian Monash University. The findings and results will be presented during the 7th International Designs for Learning Conference May 24–26, 2021 in Stockholm, Sweden. The forthcoming paper is related to the topic technology enhanced learning (TEL) and will use the multi-literacies approach as theoretical framework (Cope & Kalantzis, 2000). This epistemological approach comes from social semiotics, where teachers build a repertoire that is relevant to their subject and/or student group. The use of virtual ethnography will collect evidence of student performance through assessment activities in an online environment.

The theory that will be investigated is if visualizing learning evidence of learning based on system interaction will empower learners to actively improve learning. The objective is to integrate the Learning-by-Design pedagogy during a training program for teachers. During the online training, educational data mining of embedded assessment will be available for students in an aster plot. There will also be a rubric explaining the constructive alignment between assignment and the eight knowledge processes to foster higher order thinking skills and deeper learning.

The study is conducted with an action research approach to find remediation strategies with focus on assessment for learning. Action research is an interactive inquiry process that involves actions implemented in a workplace followed by a reflective phase to understand underlying causes, which enables future predictions about personal and organizational change. The aim is to improve the way we address issues and solve problems in the community where your practice is embedded through participatory research (Reason & Bradbury, 2001). In the background I will describe my experience of collaborative and flexible learning environments online. This has given me an understanding of digital tools and forms for online learning processes. The trends in open networked learning has now taken my journey to investigate future development of learning processes in an online environment with educational data mining. Following guiding questions will be addressed in this study:

- Q1: How can we collect data from different types of interaction in online learning environments?
- Q2: Can visualization of educational data mining be used to empower students to actively improve learning?
- Q3: What remediation strategies can be used to adjust the instruction based on the student's response to an intervention?

Background

I started EduToolkit as a grassroots organization with the purpose to facilitate "Teachers Open Online Learning for Professional Development ". The goal statement 2012 was to transform how classroom education and teachers can access the affordance of technology in their classroom. In 2020 EduToolkit has focused on the multi-literacies pedagogical approach and aspects of situated practice, critical framing, overt instruction, and transformed practice. The combination of educational data mining with peer-to-peer feedback will in the future be a valuable tool to aggregate social knowledge for learning communities.

My experience started in 2008 during an online course called "Connectivism and Connective Knowledge " (CCK08). In 2016 I enrolled in the course "Open Networked Leaning" (ONL162) and got introduced to the FISh-model an acronym for Focus, Investigate and Share (Kvarnström et al., 2015). This resonated with my previous application Learning Design Sequences (LDS) in online learning environments (Selander, 2008). I fell in love with the concept of Massive Open Online Courses (MOOC) and got inspired by the design in Open Networked Learning (ONL – https://opennetworkedlearning.wordpress.com) that used PBL-groups where the participants got agency to adapt the content and assignments required shared responsibility.

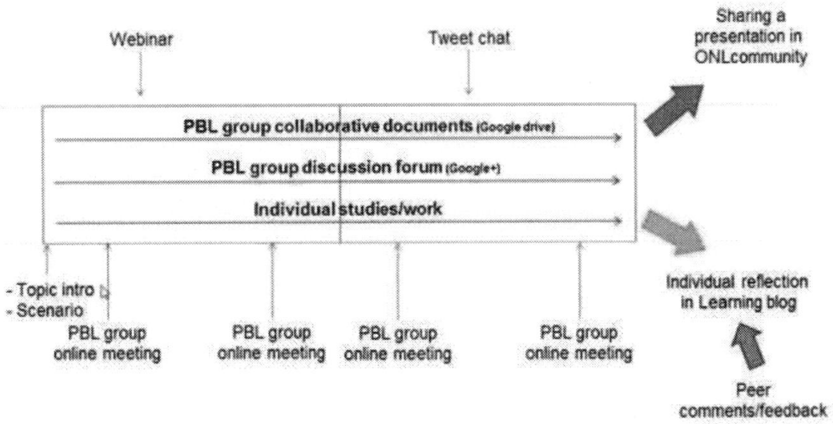

Figure 1. Design of collaborative learning in ONL181 with PBL-groups

During my reflection cycle I concluded that the challenges I saw among students was lack of motivation and not having the endurance to complete the course on schedule. The intervention I tried was to use badges and other micro-credentials to introduce gamification and developing modules that can be completed with adjustable deadlines. My conclusion was that online students are sometimes missing the ownership (i.e. means for self-regulation) and don't spontaneously share knowledge between participants (i.e. building trust). One possible explanation is that closed technologies involving "silos" and "gatekeepers" limit flexibility. My experience is that the use of a Personal Learning Environments (PLE) can shift the power balance in an online course, since the content is owned and controlled by the participant and are allowed to be used as course material. A practical example of this was in a MOOC for Swedish teachers called "Digitala Skollyftet " (www.digitalaskollyftet.se), where a blog-hub was used to harvest participants contributions on their own learning environment through syndication with RSS-feeds.

As a teacher I have used WikiEducator (www.wikieducator.org) and Wikiskola (wikiskola.se/index.php/Huvudsida) as digital tools for sharing Open Educational Resources (OER). These services are now often available in Learning Management Systems (LMS). For example, you can use commons to search for and import content into your courses in Canvas Learning Management Platform (www.instructure.com/canvas). Other repositories are linked to templates in authoring tools, like H5P (https://h5p.org) that can be used to share and reuse interactive content. Also experience API (xAPI) can be used to track data about learner actions and reports them back to a learning management system (Lim, 2015). I have often taken the approach of Distributed Cognition that address how neural networks process propagation and transformation of representations (Hutchins, 2000). This concept is practised in the connectivist MOOC with learning principles of autonomy, diversity, openness, and connectivity (Mackness et al., 2013). This line of thought also investigate the concept of rhizomatic knowledge and community as curriculum, where the learning is centred on the process of negotiation (Cormier, 2008).

Open education is no longer limited by physical and geographical constraints (i.e. ubiquitous) and allow the implementation of methods for informal assessment (i.e. Mozilla Open Badges). This has been suggested as a solution to the problem of costly higher education (Weller & Anderson, 2013).

There was also observed a new form of participation of people temporarily "sampling" the course (i.e. "drop-outs") or actively observing (i.e. "lurkers") in open learning environments (Mackness et al., 2013). Openness in education and learning is facilitated through open educational resources (OERs) and open participation in courses. I believe we are also ready for open assessment.

Case study: Integrating the Learning by Design Pedagogy in Teacher Training

To further understand how visualization of educational data mining can be used to empower students to actively improve learning there will be a case study with focus on training teachers in the learning by design pedagogy. During the summer 2020 I was a speaker at the international summer school "Modern trends in STEM Education", which was organized jointly by stakeholders and M. Auezov South Kazakhstan University. This was part of the ongoing EU funded project "Integrated Approach to STEM teacher training" that involves 10 universities from 4 EU countries and 6 universities from Russia and Kazakhstan, with objective to enhance the quality of STEM Teacher training in line with Bologna provisions and needs of knowledge economy (Välimaa & Hoffman, 2008).

Part of the deliverables are online courses and training workshops for teachers with the topic "Assessment for learning in STEM teaching". The case study that is going to be presented in this forthcoming paper is independent from the EU funded project, but will be available to participants as an online course about the Learning by Design pedagogy and incorporate the learning processes that is used in assessment for learning. The goal is also that participants build competence in educational data mining from data generated in embedded assessment. One critical aspect identified at this moment is to include all four dimensions of the multi-literacies model. If only the dimension of conceptualizing is assessed this will indicate that the learning processes are classed as traditional.

This case study will be inspired by the learning platform CG Scholar (newlearningonline.com/cgscholar) developed by educators and computer scientists at the University of Illinois. The Common Ground Scholar environment was funded 2009 by US Education Department, the Bill and Melinda Gates foundation as well as the US National Science Foundation. The community space is where course leaders post assignments and take parts in discussions with learners and the creator space allow students to improve their work based on feedback and peer-to-peer reviews before the final version is published as a "frozen" version in the publisher space in the learning portfolio. The difference to other LMS is that the performance of the student and activity in the system is utilized for learning analytics. The students are collectively building knowledge when peers write reviews, annotations, recommendations and use the checker to score requirements of other students work. I find this a good example where an evaluation of student performance also can be used in formative ways.

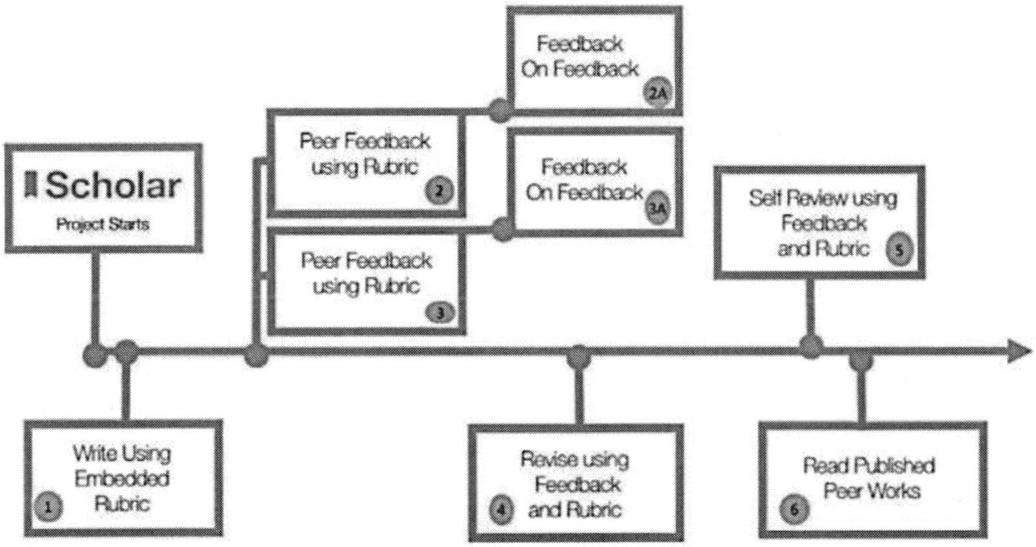

Figure 2. Course flow in CG Scholar (Source: https://youtu.be/kxd6-CIJIBI)

In CG Scholar educational data mining will let the instructor see the accumulated value of the course and the figure below shows an example of an aster plot when we are four weeks into an eight weeks course with 60 students. In this visualization we can see that 5,692 metric values as been evaluated, and 964,520 total data points collected.

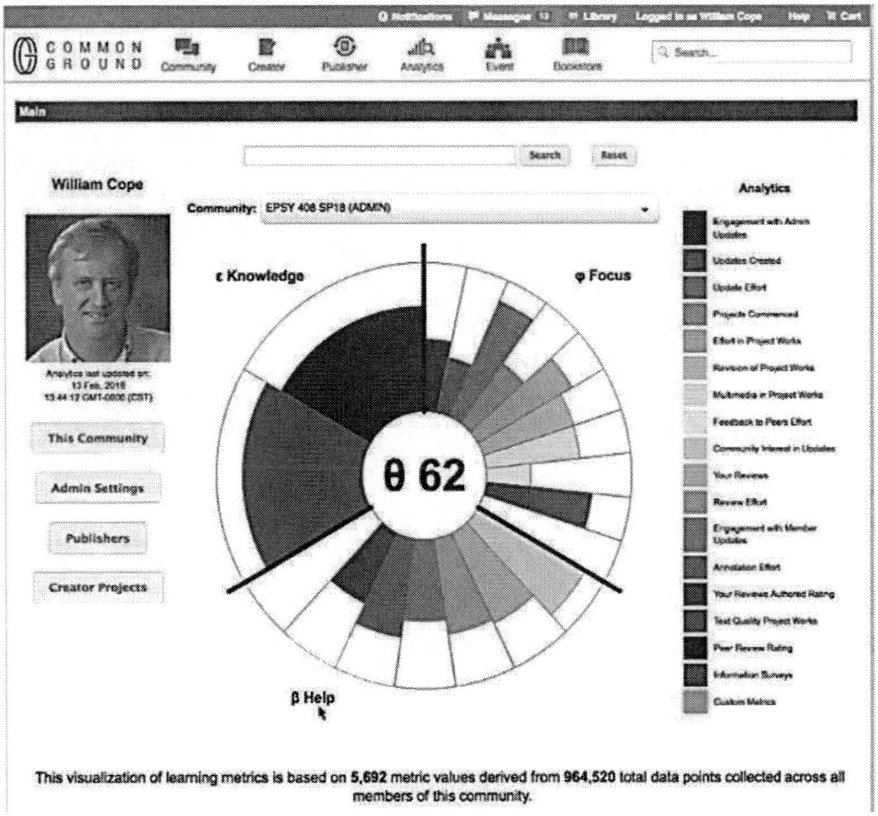

Figure 3. Example of aster plot in week 4 (Source: https://youtu.be/kxd6-CIJIBI)

There are three main sectors where focus is the amount of work the learner has done and knowledge is evidence of what has been learnt. Help is the student's collaborative relationship in this specific environment and in the centre, we can see that the group is 62% on the way to mastery. This is a concept based on the theory of Benjamin Bloom, but it is the instructor that decide what macro-categories that is measured and the weight of each expectation. The idea is that providing access to their own data will empower students to actively improve their learning.

Methodology

As explained previously action research involves testing future predictions about personal and organizational change in a real-world context. Methods for collection of data (Q1) is listed in the following table, but the scope of the case study will be limited to machine assessment that will be visualised for students in an aster plot.

Table 1: A Typology of Educational Data Sources in Computer-Mediated Learning Environments (Cope & Kalantzis, 2016; p.3).

Data type	Mode of data collection	Assessment genres: Examples
Machine assessments	Computer adaptive testing	Select response assessments, quizzes (e.g., reading comprehension, grammar, vocabulary)
Structured, embedded data	Natural language processing Procedure-defined processes Argument-defined processes Machine learning processes	Automated essay scoring, feedback on language features Games, intelligent tutors Rubric-based peer review of writing Semantic tagging and annotation, text visualizations, accepted textual change suggestions
Unstructured, incidental data	Incidental "data exhaust " Dedicated devices for collecting unstructured data	Keystroke patterns, edit histories, clickstream and navigation paths, social interaction patterns Video capture, eye trackers, movement detectors

Multi-literacy look at different dimensions of learning and we will in this study look at *Active Knowledge Making* and address *Collaborative Intelligence*. Finally we will look at the Evaluative dimension and *Recursive Feedback*. The visualization of educational data mining will be an aster plot (Q2) adjusted to the Learning-by-Design pedagogy and appendix 1 show how this is related to the multi-literacies model. This is an example of how the result will look like:

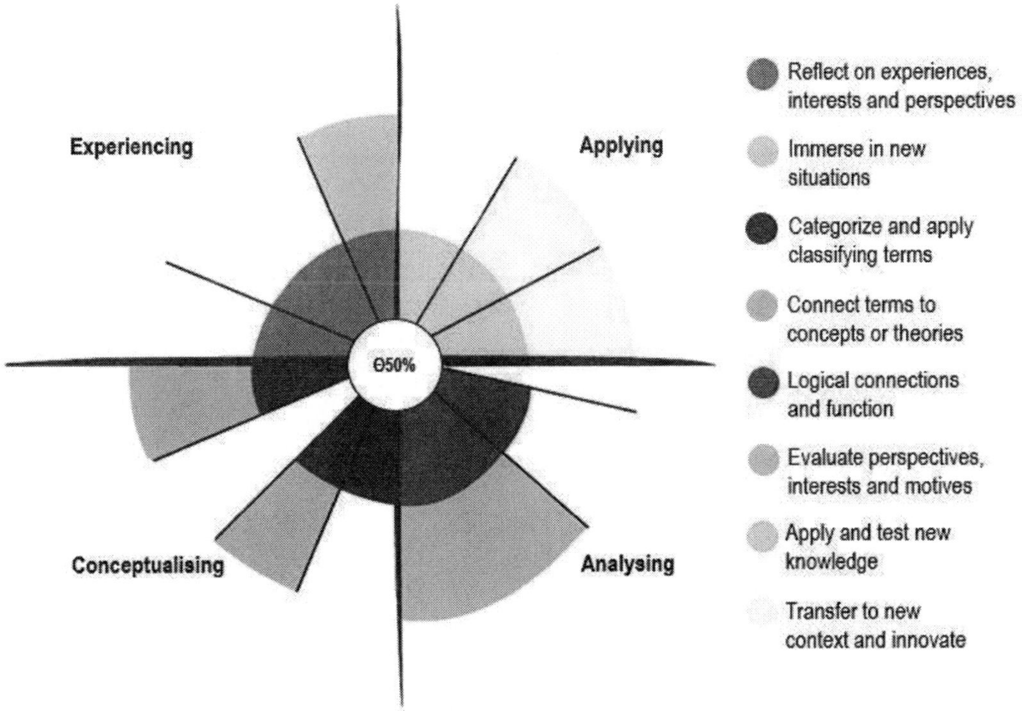

Figure 4. Aster plod illustrating the possible result of the case study

References

Cope, B., & Kalantzis, M. (2016). Big data comes to school: Implications for learning, assessment, and research. *Aera Open, 2*(2). https://doi.org/10.1177%2F2332858416641907

Cope, B., & Kalantzis, M. (Eds.). (2000). *Multiliteracies: Literacy learning and the design of social futures.* Psychology Press.

Cormier, D. (2008). Rhizomatic education: Community as curriculum. *Innovate: Journal of Online Education, 4*(5).

Hutchins, E. (2000). Distributed cognition. International Encyclopedia of the Social and Behavioral Sciences. Elsevier Science, 138.

Lim, K. C. (2015). Case studies of xAPI applications to e-Learning. *Proceedings of the 12th International Conference on eLearning for Knowledge-Based Society*, 3-1.

Kvarnström, M., Hedberg, M., Ossiannilsson, E., Åbjörnsson, L., Creelman, A., & Uhlin, L. (2015). *From awareness to participation: student engagement in an online environment.* Paper presented at the MOOCs in Scandinavia, Karolinska Institutet, Stockholm, 11-12 June 2015. Karolinska Institutet. FISh-model retrieved from https://i0.wp.com/farm6.staticflickr.com/5507/11322417494_aeceda1bdf.jpg

Mackness, J., Waite, M., Roberts, G., & Lovegrove, E. (2013). Learning in a small, task–oriented, connectivist MOOC: Pedagogical issues and implications for higher education. *International Review of Research in Open and Distributed Learning, 14*(4), 140-159.

Selander, S. (2008). Designs of learning and the formation and transformation of knowledge in an era of globalization. *Studies in Philosophy and Education, 27*(4), 267-281. Learning

Design Sequences Modell retrieved from https://www.researchgate.net/profile/Peter_Mozelius/publication/289790603/figure/fig1/AS:3164103550443 52@1452449515427/Selander-2008-processed-by-Anna-Akerfeldt-2014-Some-potential-resources-like.png

Välimaa, J., & Hoffman, D. (2008). Knowledge society discourse and higher education. *Higher Education, 56*(3), 265-285.

Waite, M., Mackness, J., Roberts, G., & Lovegrove, E. (2013). Liminal participants and skilled orienteers: Learner participation in a MOOC for new lecturers. *Journal of Online Learning and Teaching, 9*(2), 200.

Weller, M., & Anderson, T. (2013). Digital resilience in higher education. *European Journal of Open, Distance and E-Learning, 16*(1), 53.

Appendix

Appendix 1: Learning by Design and Multiliteracies Equivalences

Multiliteracies Model		Learning by Design	
Situated Practice	The immersion in experience and the utilisation of available Designs of meaning.	Experiencing	• *the known* – learners reflect on their own familiar experiences, interests and perspectives. • *the new* – learners observe or take part in something that is unfamiliar; they are immersed in new situations or contents.
Over Instruction	The systematic, analytic and conscious understanding of Designs of meaning and Design processes.	Conceptualising	• *by naming* – learners group things into categories, apply classifying terms, and define these terms. • *with theory* – learners make generalisations using concepts, and connect terms in concept maps or theories.
Critical Framing	Interpreting the social and cultural contexts, where students critically view their study topic in relation to its context.	Analysing	• *functionally* – learners analyse logical connections, cause and effect, structure and function. • *critically* – learners evaluate their own and other people's perspectives, interests and motives.
Transformed Practice	The transfer in meaning-making practice, which puts the transformed meaning to work in other contexts or cultural sites.	Applying	• *appropriately* – learners apply new learning to real world situations and test their validity. • *creatively* – learners make an intervention in the world which is innovative and creative, or transfer their learning to a different context.
Adapted from Kalanztis and Cope (2000) and New Learning Online (n.d).			

DISTANCE LEARNING AND INTERNET USE DURING THE COVID-19 PANDEMIC – THE RUSSIAN STUDENT COMMUNITY OPINION

Alina Degteva, Jenny Pange, Periklis Christou, University of Ioannina, Greece

Abstract

The COVID-19 pandemic, which is not slowing down now, has provoked changes in many social areas. University life is also changing. To assess the pandemic impact on the Russian students' lifestyle and learning, we conducted an anonymous survey with a students' random sample. Presently the study is ongoing, but the first results, obtained from July to August 2020, show that students began to use the Internet more often during the self-isolation period with different purposes. During this emergency, educational institutions liaised online with students in accessible ways, but some students reported having trouble with distance learning. We asked survey participants to predict further distance learning development and found that students believed that distance learning will be partially or completely preserved once the pandemic is over.

Keywords: COVID-19 pandemic, distance learning, Internet use, Russian students, Google Forms

Introduction

The world is currently facing an emergency caused by the Coronavirus disease (COVID-19) pandemic. According to the World Health Organization, all countries Governments have tried to protect their population from disease and in the new realities have taken measures to which citizens have had to adapt quickly. Related problems are also relevant for students.

All over the world, education is actively developing, for which it is necessary to be online as demonstrated by Marengo et al. (2012). Distance learning has supported people who have difficulty attending classes by giving them a chance to learn, according to Park and Shea (2020).

According to Shadzi et al. (2020), the Internet has become an essential and inseparable part of the modern lifestyle. With the spread of the Internet, people are more connected than ever before as demonstrated by Filsinger et al. (2020), and Marengo et al. (2013). Also, the ease of access to information of all kinds is one of the Internet main advantages, according to Toki et al. (2013), Koureta and Gasparinatou (2017), and Nikolaou et al. (2019).

In the Russian Federation, as in the rest of the world, measures have been taken for social distancing and selfisolation, according to the Russian Government. Students and academics followed the rules and accepted distance learning as the only solution to the curriculum, as stated in Butenko (2020), Kaplina (2020), and Yurchenko (2020). In addition, entertainment and communication between students have changed as demonstrated by Abramov et al. (2020), and Arzamanova (2020).

The last decade Russian studies emphasized that communication between students and teachers is most often carried out through e-mail and information from educational institutions' official websites, as stated in Shapiro (2020), and Kaplina (2020). According to Russian researchers, Ladyzhets et al. (2020) and Lutfullaev et al. (2020), not all universities during the COVID-19 quarantine period were willing to offer their students distance learning, often due to digital skills lacks and/or technological tools.

The aim of this study was to determine how the Russian student community responds to distance learning provoked by the COVID-19 pandemic, and to determine whether this format of learning and digital lifestyle has consequences.

Materials & Methods

This study target audience was Russian educational institutions' students, currently receiving higher or secondary vocational education. For the needs of this study, we asked students to fill out a questionnaire in Google Forms. A Google link to the online survey was sent to a random sample of 160 students. The link was sent to social media or via email. All participants in this study asked to convey information about this study. The poll was anonymous. The Google-linked survey has been available since early July 2020 and remains available for responses at the writing time. This paper includes data collected over 7 weeks, from July 9 until August 27, 2020. The study is currently ongoing.

In total, the questionnaire included 12 questions. The first part of questions was the demographical characteristics and included five questions (i.e. gender, age, the (city) location of the educational institution, the name of the University, and the specialization of the participants (Department in The University)).

The second part of the questionnaire consisted of six questions, which focused on the following issues:

- The amount of time that students spent daily on the Internet in self-isolation and distance learning conditions;
- The purpose of Internet use during the pandemic;
- Types of communication/interaction between students and administrative-teaching staff;
- Students' views regarding distance learning in the future;
- Problems, which faced students during this emergency.

The third part of the questionnaire was an open question, where participants were free to leave their comments about COVID-19 and distance learning or Internet use.

Results and discussion

In this study, we analysed the answers of 149 students of Russian higher or secondary vocational education educational institutions. Eleven students did not reply to our questionnaire.

Of these 149 students, 49% were males and 51% were females, whose average age was 20.3 ± 2.7 years.

The students, who took part in the study, live in six Russian cities: Saratov (83.8%), Chelyabinsk (9.4%), Moscow (3.4%), St. Petersburg (2.0%), Volgograd (0.7%), and Balakovo (0.7%).

One hundred and seventeen students indicated their educational institution they attended, namely, Yuri Gagarin State Technical University of Saratov (56.3%); N.G. Tchernyshevsky National Research University of Saratov (25.5%); Plekhanov Russian University of Economics of Saratov (0.9%); Russian Presidential Academy of National Economy and Public Administration (Balakovo (0.9%) and Volgograd (0.9%) campuses); South Urals State University (10.2%); National Research Information Technologies, Mechanics and Optics University of SaintPetersburg (0.9%); State Institute of Technology of Saint-Petersburg (0.9%); Lomonosov Moscow State University (0.9%); Timiryazev Moscow State Agrarian University (1.7%); Pedagogical State University of Moscow (0.9%).

According to our data, 54.1% of respondents studied in technical specialties, 23% of students studied the humanities, 12.2% of respondents noted that they have a natural training profile, 6.8% and 4.1% of students, respectively, studied social and applied sciences in educational institutions.

We asked all Russian students, who participated in this study, to tell us the amount of time they spent on the Internet and whether it has increased with self-isolation and distance learning. Half of the respondents (50%) noted that the time amount they spent on the Internet has increased significantly. A quarter of respondents (25.7%) believed that they started spending slightly more time online, 23% of students said that the time amount they spent online remained unchanged, and only 1.4% of respondents thought that they started spending less time online during the pandemic.

Then, we asked the students to calculate how much time they spent on the Internet every day during self-isolation. There are 42.2% of respondents reported that they were online for 4-6 hours daily, 22.1% of students said that they spent 7-9 hours on the Internet daily, 16.4% of survey participants talked about numbers in the range of 10-12 hours, 15% of students emphasized that they used the Internet only 1-3 hours a day. On the other hand, 4.3% of respondents reported that they spent 13-15 hours online every day.

The students indicated that the purposes they used the Internet during a pandemic were, for education (85.9%), for entertainment (85.2%), for communication (76.5%), for self-development, including online sports training, foreign language classes and so forth (73.2%), and for work (40.3%).

In our questionnaire, we asked students to clarify how the administrative and teaching staff contacted students in the spring semester quarantine. Our data suggest that the most preferred communication methods for educational workers were video conferencing (87.9%), e-mail (80.5%), the educational organization official website (71.1%), and social networks (64.4%).

We also asked students for their views on maintaining distance learning after this emergency. There are 53% of students believed that distance learning will be partially or completely continue after the pandemic ends, 20.8% of respondents believed that distance learning will end with this emergency end, and 26.2% of students did not reply.

It was important for the study to determine what problems the students faced during the distance learning caused by the pandemic. So 41.6% of students reported that it was difficult for them to get too much information, 33.6% of respondents noted that they did not have enough communication with peers and/or administrative-teaching staff, 24.2% of students had anxiety about the future, 18.1% of respondents said they lacked technical support, and 5.4% of students commented on digital skills lack. Meanwhile, 25.5% of respondents reported that they did not face the above problems.

In the final question, students expressed their opinion on distance learning and COVID-19. Many students said that it was more difficult faculty members to adapt to distance learning than for students, and they wanted clear instructions from academics. The survey participants also noticed that the attitude towards distance learning is subjective. The students emphasized that it takes a long time to get used to fully online education and that this education form has both pros and cons. Other respondents expressed their opinion that traditional education is more preferable for them.

Conclusions

According to this study, half of the students surveyed were faced with the fact that during the pandemic they began to spend significantly more time on the Internet. The main purpose for them to work in the Internet was education, or entertainment, or communication.

Most of the students surveyed believed that distance learning will be partially or completely preserved after the pandemic is over. During this emergency, educational institutions most often offered survey participants to communicate by video communication, e-mail, the educational organization official website and social networks means. Also, according to our data, students during the self-isolation period provoked by the COVID-19 pandemic more often than others faced problems associated with an incoming information large amount, communication lack, and anxiety about the future. Few students surveyed reported a technical support lack and/or digital skills.

Our findings revealed that in the 21st century, the Internet has become an essential and indispensable tool for studying during emergencies such as a pandemic, as well as for personal needs, including entertainment, information search and communication. Since emergencies are usually unpredictable, it is prudent to prioritize distance learning at universities for the quality education. Therefore, it is very important universities to plan more online courses for their students, educational webinars, online conferences, as well as develop innovative approaches to the procedure for testing the acquired knowledge.

References

Abramov, A. V., Bagdasaryan, V. E., Byshok, S. O., Volodenkov, S. V., Evstafev, D. G., & Egorov, V. G. (2020). COVID19 Pandemic: the end of the familiar world? *Bulletin of the Regional State University of Moscow, 2*, 3-83. doi:10.18384/2224-0209-2020-2-1001

Arzamanova, T. (2020). First lessons of the first pandemic of the 21 century. *European security: Events, Assessments, Forecasts, 57*(73), 2-12. Retrieved from https://www.elibrary.ru/download/elibrary_43167197_58581216.pdf

Butenko, E. D. (2020). COVID-19 as a shock stimulating factor in the development of digital education. *Management in Economic and Social systems, 2*(4), 19-27. Retrieved from https://www.elibrary.ru/download/elibrary_43130564_55068337.pdf

Filsinger, M., Ackermann, K., & Freitag, M. (2020). Surfing to help? An empirical analysis of Internet use and volunteering in 27 European societies. *European Societies Journal, 22*(3), 368-389. Retrieved from https://www.tandfonline.com/doi/abs/10.1080/14616696.2019.1663895

Kaplina, S. E. (2020, June). *Education in the COVID-19 Pandemic.* Paper presented at the "New Science: past, present, future" Conference, Ufa, Russia. Retrieved from https://www.elibrary.ru/download/elibrary_43055858_74835488.pdf

Koureta, M., & Gasparinatou, A. (2017, November). *Factors that Motivate or Discourage Postgraduate Students during the Process of Writing Assignments in Distance Learning Education.* Paper presented at the 9th International Conference in Open & Distance Learning, Athens, Greece. Retrieved from https://www.researchgate.net/publication/322811938_Paragontes_pou_energopoioun_e_a potharrynoun_tous_ekp aideuomenous_kata_ten_ekponese_ton_GE_sten_ex_apostaseos_ekpaideuse

Ladyzhets, N. S., Neborsky, E. V., Boguslavsky, M. V., & Naumova, T. A. (2020). Social and educational aspects of force majeure actualization of theory and practice of digital university under the conditions of COVID-19 pandemic. *Bulletin of Udmurt University. Sociology. Political Science. International Relationships, 4*(2), 125-131. doi:10.35634/2587-9030-2020-4-2-125-131

Lutfullaev, G. U., Lutfullaev, U. L., Kobilova, Sh. Sh., & Neimatov, U. S. (2020). Experience of distance learning during COVID-19 pandemic. *Problems of Pedagogy, 4*(49), 66-69. Retrieved from https://elibrary.ru/download/elibrary_43077399_81439645.pdf

Marengo, A., Pagano, A., & Barbone, A. (2012, June). *Adaptive Learning: A New Approach in Student Modeling.* Paper presented at the International Conference on Information Technology Interfaces, ITI, Dubrovnik, Croatia. Retrieved from https://dblp.org/db/conf/iti/iti2012.html

Marengo, A., Pagano, A., & Barbone, A. (2013, May). *Data Mining Methods to Assess Student Behavior in Adaptive Elearning Processes.* Paper presented at the 4th International Conference on e-Learning Best Practices in Management, Design and Development of e-Courses: Standards of Excellence and Creativity, ECONF 2013, Manama, Bahrain. Retrieved from https://ieeexplore.ieee.org/document/6745564

Park, H., & Shea, P. (2020). A review of ten-year research through co-citation analysis: online learning, distance learning, and blended learning. *Online Learning Journal, 24*(2), 225-244. Retrieved from https://files.eric.ed.gov/fulltext/EJ1260330.pdf

Shadzi, M. R., Salehi, A., & Vardanjani, H. M. (2020). Problematic Internet use, mental health, and sleep quality among medical students: a path-analytic model. *Indian Journal of Psychological Medicine, 2*(42), 128-135. Retrieved from https://journals.sagepub.com/doi/pdf/10.4103/IJPSYM.IJPSYM_238_19

Shapiro, N. A. (2020, May). *Pandemic COVID-19 as Destruction Factor Educational Routines.* Paper presented at the "Modern society: problems, contradictions, solutions" Conference, St. Petersburg, Russia. Retrieved from https://elibrary.ru/item.asp?id=43055423

Sousal, R., Nikolaou, V., Karayiannis, R., Plakitsi, K., & Pange, J. (2019, March). *A comparison of ICT Use in Greece and Portugal.* Paper presented at the ISCAR Regional Conference 2019, Ioannina, Greece. Retrieved from http://iscar2019.conf.uoi.gr/

The Russian Government official website (2020). Measures of the Government of the Russian Federation to combat coronavirus infection and support the economy. Retrieved from http://government.ru/support_measures/

Toki, E., Sypsas, A., Pange, A., & Pange, J. (2013, November). *E-learning and Webinars: Teachers' and Students' Views.* Paper presented at the 7th International Conference in Open & Distance Learning, Athens, Greece. Retrieved from https://www.academia.edu/23551575/%CE%95_learning_and_Webinars_Teachers_and_students_views

World Health Organization (2020). Country & Technical Guidance – Coronavirus disease (COVID-19). Retrieved from https://www.who.int/emergencies/diseases/novel-coronavirus-2019/technical-guidance

Yurchenko, S. G. (2020). New tasks of quality management of remote education in the conditions of higher ready mode (COVID-19). *Bulletin of the Scientific-Methodological Council for Natural Development and Water Use, 18*(18), 13-25. Retrieved from https://www.elibrary.ru/download/elibrary_43808550_37963998.pdf

INTERNAL QUALITY ASSURANCE THROUGH MODEL VALIDATION RESEARCH: DEVELOPMENT OF A COMPREHENSIVE VALIDATION INVENTORY TOOL FOR INSTRUCTIONAL DESIGN MODELS FOR DISTANCE EDUCATION

Jennalyn Tayam, University of the Philippines – Diliman, Philippines

Abstract

Despite the use of instructional design principles in the plan, design, development, and implementation of distance education instructional design models, there is an inadequacy of studies utilizing the assessment, validation and evaluation principles that the instructional design discipline offers. This study utilizes model validation research in order to develop a comprehensive validation inventory tool for instructional design models for distance education.

Keywords: Remote learning, Instructional design model quality assurance, Assessment tool, Validation instrument

Introduction

Internal quality assurance in distance education is defined as the dimension of quality assurance that deals with "internal continuous improvement" (Scull, Kendrick, Shearer, & Offerman, 2011). It ensures that all of an institution's efforts for distance education has led to a positive and high quality experience for the target learners (Thorpe, 2003). Internal quality assurance holds instructional design as one of its core components, since instructional design principles, such as design, development, and implementation, are usually applied and further studied to determine the best practices for course design in distance education (Zawacki-Richter & Naidu, 2016).

However, the application of instructional design principles in distance education has three undesirable themes predominant in literature (Southard & Mooney, 2015): (a) the unresolved questions on the effectiveness, validity and reliability of instructional design models (Branch & Kopcha, 2013), (b) the inadequate funding devoted to instructional design research (Jung, 2005), and (c) the limited utilization of instructional design-evaluation processes (Zhang, & Cheng, 2012). Dwelling further on the issue of the scarcity of instructional-design evaluation research in distance education is the discovery that the utilization of comprehensive model validation research principles in instructional design models for distance learning is almost nil (Branch & Kopcha, 2013; Richey, Klein, & Nelson, 2009). This is despite the fact that the assessment of distance-education through valid methods and tools should be the type of quality assurance that should receive most of the attention and effort of educators and researchers (Scull et al., 2011).

Due to the presented undesirable themes in the literature, the development of inventory tools which will aid the comprehensive model validation process for distance education is deemed as necessary. In order to develop an inventory tool that could be used to comprehensively validate instructional design models for distance education, this study employed the Delphi method (Habibi, Sarafrazi, & Izadyar, 2014), specifically, a modified Delphi method, which has two parts: (a) a systematic literature review and (b) the Delphi iterations/experts' review (Avella, 2016). This is so that the need to gather "theory and practice" data, demanded by both distance education and instructional design researches, could be addressed (York & Ertmer, 2011; Richey & Klein, 2007; Shale, 2003).

Research Questions

The goal of this study is to construct a comprehensive inventory tool for validating instructional design models for distance education, using a modified Delphi method. Specifically, it seeks to answer the following questions:

- What are the measurable indicators for validating instructional design models for distance education, in terms of the components of comprehensive model validation?
- What is the structure and form of a comprehensive inventory tool for validating instructional design models for distance education?
- Is the developed inventory tool agreed upon, collectively, by the panel of experts?

Theoretical Framework

The theoretical framework for this research is presented in Figure 1. The theoretical framework shows the philosophical, epistemological, methodological, and analytical foundations of which the researcher approached this study (Grant & Osanloo, 2014). A Venn diagram is used to represent the core relationships of the three variables that constitutes the construct of the study, in order to show how the concepts that could be found separately in each variables could be combined to solve the research problem (Verdinelli & Scagnoli, 2013).

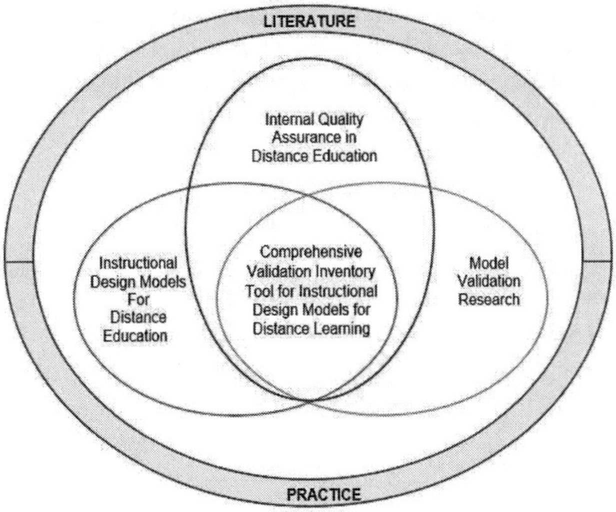

Figure 1. Theoretical framework of the study

Methodology

Research Procedure

A modified Delphi method, which has two parts: (a) a systematic literature review and (b) the Delphi iterations/experts' review, is used in this study; a summary of the procedure is presented in Figure 2.

The research procedure is adapted from the theoretical framework for conventional Delphi method as proposed by Habibi, Sarafrazi, and Izadyar (2014), modified and incorporated with the findings of Avella (2016), Heale and Forbes (2013), Pare et al. (2013), von der Gracht (2012) and Hsu and Sandford (2007). Since this study aims for the consensus of the panel members in the elements and characteristics of a comprehensive instructional design model inventory tool, it will use rating scales not ranking orders, thus, the narrowing phase that Pare et al. (2013) will not be used. All the items in the first and second round questionnaires (Q1, Q2) will be included for rating in the Reach Consensus Phase (Phase 3); no items will be removed from the list even if consensus for the said item has been achieved (Hsu & Sandford, 2007).

Phase 1: Plan

The study will use purposive sampling to gather the opinion of 40 experts, since it requires information from specific individuals who are involved in distance education (20 experts) and instructional design validation processes (20 experts) (Brady, 2015; Paré et al., 2013). The study has no specific location since the panel of experts will be selected based on expertise and will be contacted via electronic means (Avella, 2016; Zeedick, 2010).

As for the inclusion criteria for the panel members, they should have a PhD degree OR has six (6) years of experience in or related to the following: (a) remote or distance education/learning, instructional design, tool development/assessment and evaluation; and (b) should be knowledgeable about or involved in the status of internal quality assurance, specifically of what measurable indicators should be included in an inventory tool that aims to validate instructional design models for distance learning.

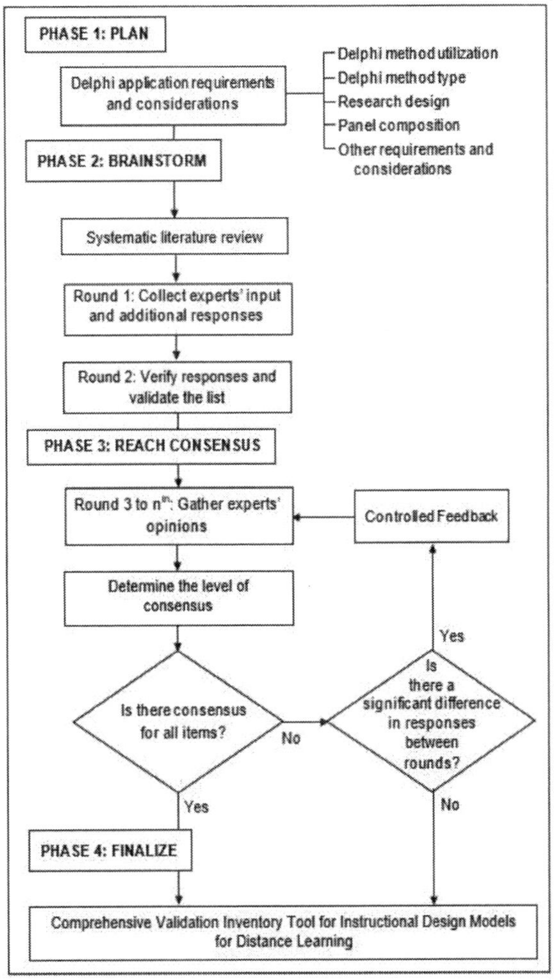

Figure 2. Summary of research procedure

Phase 2: Brainstorm

Systematic literature review

In this study, a systematic literature review will be conducted as the Delphi modification, in order to generate an initial list of items that answers the research problem. The systematic literature review steps (Hart, 2018) has been modified and aligned with the brainstorming part of the modified Delphi method. An eligibility or inclusion criteria that will filter and sort out the literature has been developed (Table 1). Structural coding (Saldaña 2009), aided by a computer-assisted qualitative analysis software (CAQDAS), ATLAS.ti, will be used to synthesize and analyse the data gathered from the systematic literature review (Woods, Paulus, Atkins, & Macklin, 2016).

Table 1: Systematic literature review inclusion criteria

Criterion Type	Inclusion Criteria
Topic	Elements and characteristics of an inventory tool that validates instructional design models for distance education, along the parameters of distance education internal quality assurance and model validation research
Publication Type	Any

Publication Date	2000 - 2020
Research Design	Must apply sound, logical methodology explicitly stated in the study; used appropriate methods and tools (if applicable)
Language	Any (as long as could be translated in English via Google, etc.)

Delphi iterations (Expert review)

The implementation of the Delphi method includes the design and implementation of questionnaires and the analysis of feedback; it is expected that a pattern of utilizing the same methods of gathering and analysing data will be observed throughout the research procedure (Crawford & Wright, 2016):

- The first round questionnaire (Q1) will be developed from the results of the systematic literature review. Q1 will be used (a) to ask the experts to rate the significance of each item generated, using a seven-point Likert scale; and (b) to gather information from the panel members about whether to add to the list of items or suggest the removal of an item, based on their own knowledge (Brady, 2015).
- The second round questionnaire (Q2) will be developed from the results of the analysis of the responses Q1. The panel members will also validate the contents of Q2, finalizing the list of items (Paré et al., 2013).
- The third round questionnaire (Q3) will be developed through using the data gathered from the finalization and validation of Q2.
- The fourth to the nth round questionnaire (Q4 to Qn) will be developed based on the results gathered from the questionnaire that preceded them, e.g. data from Q3 will be used to design Q4, and so on.

The methodological considerations for the Delphi iterations (experts' review) are presented in Table 2.

Table 2: Methodological considerations for the Delphi iterations (expert review)

Methodological Consideration	Description
Turnover period	The earliest possible return of the each questionnaire is within seven days (one week) and the latest would be within 14 days.
Updates	Follow up e-mails will be done twice: on the 7th day and on the 12th day.
Response rate	When the response rate of 90% has been achieved and the remaining panel of experts do not respond anymore, the results will be subjected to analysis.
Quantitative data analysis	Results from the Likert scale responses, will be analysed through calculating the median and the interquartile range.
Qualitative data analysis	Results from the open-ended questions will be analysed through structural coding (Saldaña, 2009), aided by ATLAS.ti (Woods et al., 2016).

Phase 3: Reach consensus

If all the items acquire a high consensus, the Delphi rounds could be terminated and the researcher could move to Phase 4: Finalize (Schmidt, 1997, as cited in Habibi et al., 2014). If the given consensus criteria is not achieved, another statistical analysis which will establish whether there is a significant difference with the results gathered from two successive rounds will be calculated: the Wilcoxon matched-pairs signed rank test. Thus, if there are items where the panel members have not reached a consensus yet and the response stability is significant, the study could move on to the fourth (to the nth round). However, if the response stability is not significant, the rounds could be terminated and the study could move to Phase 4: Finalize (Schmidt, 1997, as cited in Habibi et al., 2014).

Phase 4: Finalize

When it is established and made clear that a consensus has already been achieved or that there is no more significant difference in the response stability, the Delphi rounds will be terminated. This is the end of the study and will show the final output. The researcher will develop a document presenting the final result, which will be sent to the panel members, along with a letter of gratitude for their contribution.

Anticipated Output

The anticipated output of the study is a "theory and practice"-based, expert-validated comprehensive validation inventory tool for instructional design models for distance education.

References

Avella, J. (2016). Delphi panels: Research design, procedures, advantages, and challenges. *International Journal of Doctoral Studies, 11*, 305-321.

Brady, S. (2015). Utilizing and adapting the Delphi method for use in qualitative research. *International Journal of Qualitative Methods, 1*(6). doi:10.1177/1609406915621381

Crawford, M., & Wright, G. (2016). *Delphi method.* Wiley StatsRef: Statistics Reference Online. John Wiley & Sons, Ltd.

von der Gracht, H. A. (2012). Consensus measurement in Delphi studies. *Technological Forecasting and Social Change, 79*(8), 1525-1536. doi:10.1016/j.techfore.2012.04.013

Grant, C., & Osanloo, A. (2014). *Understanding, selecting, and integrating a theoretical framework in dissertation research: Creating the blueprint for your "house".* doi:10.5929/2014.4.2.9

Habibi, A., Sarafrazi, A., Izadyar, S. (2014). Delphi technique theoretical framework in qualitative research. *The International Journal of Engineering and Science, 3*(4), 8-13

Hart, C. (2018). *Doing a literature review: Releasing the research imagination.* Sage.

Hsu, C., & Sandford, B. (2007). The Delphi technique: Making sense of consensus. *Practical Assessment, Research and Evaluation, 12*, 1-8.

Jung, I. (2005). Quality assurance survey of mega universities. In C. McIntosh & Z. Varoglu (Eds.), *Perspectives on Distance Education: Lifelong Learning and Distance Higher Education* (pp. 79-98). COL, UNESCO. Retrieved from https://unesdoc.unesco.org/ark:/48223/pf0000141218

Paré, G., Cameron, A.-F., Poba-Nzaou, P., & Templier, M. (2013). A systematic assessment of rigor in information systems ranking-type Delphi studies. *Information & Management, 50*(5), 207-217.

Reigeluth, C., & Carr-Chellman, A. (Eds.) (2009). *Instructional-design theories and models: Building a common knowledge base* (Vol. III). New York: Routledge.

Richey, R. C., & Klein, J. D. (2007). *Design and development research: Methods, strategies, and issues.* New York: Routledge.

Richey, R. Klein, J., & Nelson, W. (2009). *Design and development research: Methods, strategies, and issues.* New York: Routledge.

Saldaña, J. (2009). *The coding manual for qualitative researchers.* Sage Publications Ltd.

Scull, W. R., Kendrick, D., Shearer, R., Offerman, D. (2011). The Landscape of Quality Assurance in Distance Education. *Continuing Higher Education Review, 75*, 138-149.

Shale, D. (2003). Performance indicators and quality assessment. In Panda, S. (Ed.), *Planning and management in distance education.* London: Routledge.

Southard, S., & Mooney, M. (2015). A comparative analysis of distance education quality assurance standards. *Quarterly Review of Distance Education, 16*(1), 55.

Thorpe, M. (2003). External control and internal quality assurance. In Panda, S. (Ed.), *Planning and Management in Distance Education.* London: Routledge.

Verdinelli, S., & Scagnoli, N. I. (2013). Data Display in Qualitative Research. *International Journal of Qualitative Methods, 12*(1), 359-381. doi:10.1177/160940691301200117

Woods, M., Paulus, T., Atkins, D. P., & Macklin, R. (2016). Advancing Qualitative Research Using Qualitative Data Analysis Software (QDAS)? Reviewing Potential Versus Practice in Published Studies using ATLAS.ti and NVivo, 1994–2013. *Social Science Computer Review, 34*(5), 597-617. https://doi.org/10.1177/0894439315596311

York, C., & Ertmer, P. (2011). Towards an understanding of instructional design heuristics: An exploratory Delphi study. *Educational Technology Research and Development, 43*(4), 60-70.

Zawacki-Richter, O., & Naidu, S. (2016). Mapping research trends from 35 years of publications in Distance Education. *Distance Education, 37*(3), 245-269.

Zeedick, D. (2010). *The modified Delphi method to analyze the application of instructional design theory to online graduate education.* USA: ProQuest LLC

Zhang, W., & Cheng, Y. (2012). Quality Assurance in E-Learning: PDPP Evaluation Model and its Application. *International Review of Research in Open and Distributed Learning, 13*(3), 66-82. . https://doi.org/10.19173/irrodl.v13i3.1181

TEACHER TRAINING THROUGH ARGUMENTATION TO PROMOTE AUTONOMOUS LEARNING IN EDUCATIONAL ENVIRONMENTS MEDIATED BY TECHNOLOGY

Larisa Enríquez Vázquez, Myrna Hernández Gutiérrez, Universidad Nacional Autónoma de México, Mexico

Abstract

One of the current and most relevant problems in the contemporary context is the lack of autonomy in the learning process. This problem is identified by all participants of the Autonomous Learning Seminar who agree that it is important to address the problem from the perspective of research, management, and above all, from the didactics both for teachers and students. To address this situation, in 2020 we wanted to approach the study of autonomous learning from a broad perspective but mainly, with the intention of promoting among teachers a different attitude that enhances at the same time, a different attitude towards students and that strengthen the development of the different dimensions that make up autonomous learning. The following work presents the preliminary results of the teachers' formative experience applying an argumentation model to provoke reflection, dialogue and self-criticism of their work carried out, in the development of the autonomy of their own students.

Keywords: Teacher training, autonomous learning, written argumentation, ideas card.

Introduction

The Open University, Educational Innovation and Distance Education Coordination of the National Autonomous University of Mexico, has a research area around autonomous learning to study its different aspects; it is the Autonomous Learning Laboratory (ALL). One of the laboratory's main functions is teacher training. In order to contribute to the training and updating of the university's faculties, the ALL organizes, among other academic events, an annual seminar. In 2020 the topic addressed in the seminar is "Dimensions of Autonomous Learning" and it involves researchers, teachers, students, as well as those responsible for open and distance programs, interested in studying problems and topics related to educational systems in alternative modes to those that happen in campus.

The seminar has had a formative character focused on teacher training. From this space, teachers have been supported to recognize issues and problems that surround education; in particular distance education and technology-mediated education. Being a formative event, these issues are addressed not only at a theoretical level but also at an experimental level derived from their application in the teaching - learning process in general and in the teaching practice of the participants involved in particular.

Autonomy

The interest for the study of autonomy is not recent. Over the years, different topics have been investigated. Littlewood (1996), referring to learner autonomy, defined two main components: "capacity and will". Capacity depends on having knowledge about the alternatives from which decisions should be made and the necessary skills to carry out the choices that seem more appropriate; will depends on having both, the motivation and the confidence to take responsibility for the required choices.

More recently, speaking of autonomous learning, Manrique (2004) defines it as the capacity that a person has to direct, control, regulate and evaluate their way of learning, consciously and intentionally making use of learning strategies to achieve the desired objective or goal. This autonomy must be the ultimate goal of education, which is expressed in knowing learning to learn. For Tassinari (2010), the students' autonomy is the meta-capacity that students possess to take control of their learning process to different degrees and in different ways, depending on their particular learning situation. The autonomy of the apprentice is a complex construction, a construction of constructions, involving several dimensions and components.

Although the study of learning indicates that it is essential that students develop awareness of the importance of recognizing that learning is a process that can be improved and that there are specific actions that will help them do it; we consider that the participation of the teacher in this process is also essential.

Gruendel, referring to Littlewood, points out that "... since learning arises from interaction and interaction is characterized by interdependence, the development of autonomy in students presupposes the development of autonomy in teachers" (Gruendel, 2018; p.142). Reinders and Balcikanli (2011) point out that it is necessary that, to train autonomous students, teachers themselves must understand what autonomous learning is as well as develop skills and strategies for it. Gruendel herself indicates some elements as ways in which teachers can promote student autonomy; in particular it refers to dialogue and inquiry, dialogue and reflection, proactive and continuous development of teacher autonomy and motivation.

The question that arises then is, can teachers be trained to promote these elements:

- Do teachers, as students, exercise such actions?

Given the unquestionable importance of autonomy in learning and with the intention of promoting among teachers a different position that at the same time promotes a different attitude towards students and strengthens the development of the various dimensions that make up autonomous learning, in the 2020 issue of the Autonomous learning seminar, it was decided to address the issue based on the dimensions proposed by Tassinari in her dynamic model of learner autonomy (Tassinari, 2012).

Tassinari's Dynamic model of learner autonomy

Tassinari's dynamic autonomous learning model is a tool designed to support self-assessment of learning competencies in order to help students and teachers focus on relevant aspects of the learning process. The dynamic model accounts for the dimensions of autonomous learning: cognitive, metacognitive, action-oriented, social and affective; and provides descriptors of the attitudes, skills and behaviours expected for learners for each of the dimensions. This model is dynamic in order to allow learners to focus on their own needs and goals. Table 1 presents the five dimensions with their corresponding objectives.

Table 1: Autonomous learning dimensions

Dimensions	Objectives
Affective	Development of attitudes, disposition, preparation, self-confidence (derived from an intrinsic motivation and activation of metacognitive strategies).
Social	Willingness to work cooperatively (derived from intrinsic motivation and activation of cognitive strategies).
Metacognitive	Definition of goals and planning (derived from an intrinsic motivation). Activation of strategies (focused on being a better learner). Monitoring (monitoring and self-assessment of progressive achievements). Internal reflection (own assessment of the results obtained).
Cognitive	Definition of goals and planning (derived from an intrinsic motivation). Activation of strategies (focused on learning more about a particular topic). Monitoring (monitoring and self-assessment of progressive achievements). Self-evaluation (own assessment of the results obtained).
Action oriented	Taking decisions, activation of skills and learning behaviours.

DDS Model

The ability to argue is one of the necessary skills in this new century; Learning to learn requires this competence and its development is necessary for both teachers and students in order to have a dialogic approach between both of them. As Karlsson et al. mention, this exercise helps students build an internal dialogue with their learning (Karlsson et al., 2007; p.53). In order to develop the ability to argue during the seminar, it was decided that the way of working would be based on the Dialogue Design System (DDS) model by Makino in 2009.

DDS is based on Toulmin's argumentation model and uses a resource called Ideas card as a didactic support; in them the students solve the theses proposed by the teacher and it is through this iterative process that the strengthening of argumentative capacities in the students is promoted. The procedure for applying the model is as follows:

1. The professor presents a thesis related to a topic.
2. Students determine if the thesis is true or false, present the arguments and evidence that supports their position, on the Ideas card.
3. The teacher evaluates the Ideas card.
4. The teacher presents the general results obtained to the group, emphasizing main arguments and counterarguments that were presented in the Ideas card.
5. The students collectively construct a guided dialogue, which gives theoretical support, in a broad way, to the object of study.
6. The teacher summarizes the discussions and suggests a general result of the dialogue. Each student receive their own Ideas card back with specific feedback on their argumentation.

Argumente

One of the ALL's developments is the *Argumente* online system. It is an Internet-based software whose objective is to automate DDS. This computer system was developed within a student-centred teaching framework; as Reyes and Moreno (2016) point out, student-centred teaching is a form of teaching in which students acquire a more active role, with greater responsibilities in the process and the teacher; instead of just delivering information, teacher becomes a guide for learning, which enhances his or hers role to teach people. This paradigm shift involves the use of a variety of teaching and assessment methods. Along with learning information, students learn to use it in a context to solve problems and acquire autonomy to acquire new information in the future. The goal of student-centred teaching is to create learning environments that optimize opportunities for students to pay attention and actively participate in authentic, meaningful, and useful learning (Figure 1. *Argumente*).

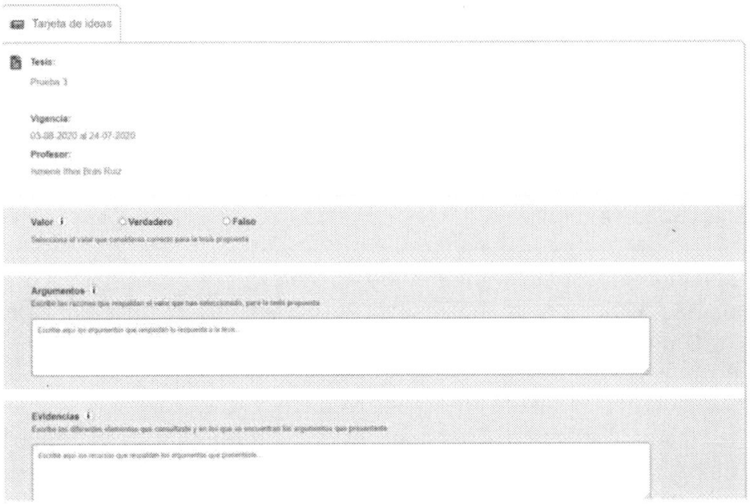

Figure 1. Ideas card in *Argumente*

Ongoing experience

Based on this procedure, the seminar's way of working was designed, aimed at achieving the objective that the participants develop their ability to argue, while discussing the selected topics and the dimensions of autonomous learning.

The ongoing work has the following characteristics: the seminar is offered in an online mode, so a website is used in which the materials for the month are published; they will help prepare the arguments related to the triggering thesis. Participants have three weeks to elaborate and write down their arguments in *Argumente*; coordinators evaluate the Ideas cards and organize them during the fourth week to present them in the monthly session. The monthly meeting is held by videoconference and in it a debate and conclusions session is held, taking up arguments, counterarguments and evidence that were registered in *Argumente*.

The didactic planning of the seminar considers that participants deliver a final product that consists of a solution proposed to a teaching problem addressed or an intervention in which the teacher promotes autonomous learning in his or her practice.

To address the concept of autonomous learning, it was decided to use Tassinari's dynamic model for learner autonomy and its five dimensions, which are studied based on specific issues that the teacher faces in practice. In this way, to address each of the dimensions, a thesis linked with a current educational issues is proposed for each dimension in order to reflect on the teaching and student work towards the specific topic. Table 2 shows the relationship between dimensions, topics and thesis.

Table 2: Relation between topics, thesis and dimensions

Dimension	Topic	Thesis
Metacognitive	Evaluation in distance education	There are no reliable evaluation methods in distance education
Cognitive	Adaptive learning	An autonomous student does not need a teacher to learn
Emotional	Problem-based learning	Project Based Learning generates motivation in students
Social	Collaborative learning	All people have the ability to collaborate
Action-oriented	Tools that promote autonomy	Communication is a fundamental tool for autonomy

Preliminary results

The Seminar is still ongoing; at the moment only three of the five dimensions of the model have been worked on. An evaluation of the results is carried out in different ways that include quantitative and qualitative evaluation.

The quantitative evaluation is linked to aspects related to the teachers' attitudes towards the work designed for them. The way teachers get involved through the resolution of the thesis is analysed considering the number of bibliographic references that they look and that are not those suggested by the project coordinators. In addition, the number of people who promote dialogue and analysis is counted, through new theses, questions and reflections that they incorporate in the idea cards, in the "Doubts" section. The improvement in the quality of the argumentation is also evaluated, through the marks that each teacher obtains on their Ideas card.

For the qualitative evaluation, specific arguments provided by teachers for the different theses were analysed, considering the link with autonomous learning and teaching practice. Table 3 shows that, although the permanence of the participants was somewhat reduced, people who have continued attending the seminar have improved their engagement with the activities.

Table 3: Quantitative results

Thesis	Solved Ideas cards	Percentage of teachers who consult other references	Group average number of additional bibliographic references	Percentage of teachers adding doubts	Group average rating in the quality of the argumentation
There are no reliable evaluation methods in distance education.	30	76%	2.65	55%	3.62
A self-employed learner does not need a teacher to learn	17	100%	4.17	60%	4.29
Project Based Learning generates motivation in students	15	86%	4.38	70%	4.53

Graph 1 shows that there has been an improvement in the quality of the argumentation, which is considered to be the result of the fact that the number of sources reviewed has also increased.

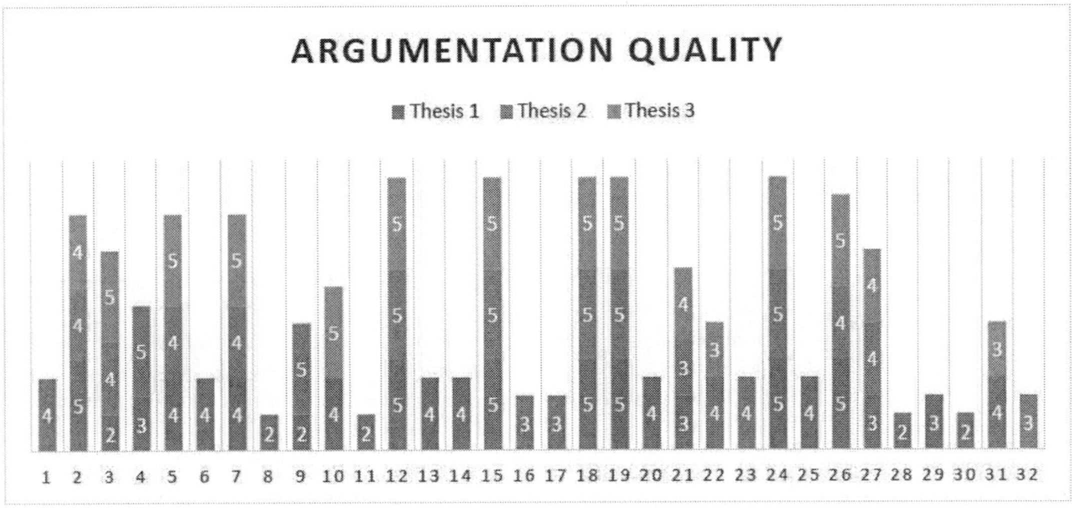

Graph 1. Argumentation quality

Likewise, it can be deduced that, derived from the increase in the number of additional sources that each participant has reviewed, more doubts and reflections arise that are not only raised in the work of the Ideas cards, but also in the active participation in the synchronous sessions (see Graph 2).

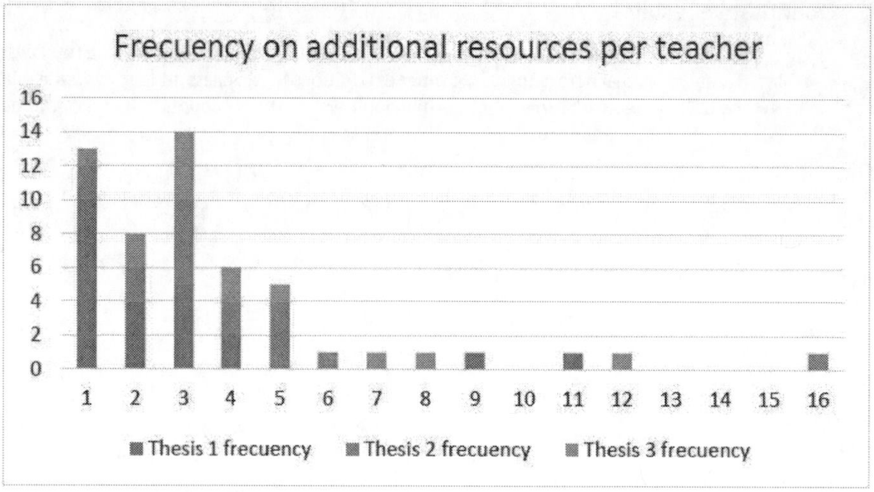

Graph 2. Frequency on additional resources reviewed by teachers

As for the qualitative evaluation, the comments we have about the work and discussion around each thesis is summarize in Table 4.

Table 4: Comments on teachers' development

Thesis	Comments throughout the synchronous session
There are no reliable remote assessment methods	Teachers do not know non-formal logic, so it was difficult for them to take a position when working on the first thesis.
	The conclusion of the first thesis was that continuous evaluation is a reliable method to evaluate in distance education; this type of evaluation is more reliable and includes the kind of feedback that the development of autonomy requires.
	It is preferred to carry out the evaluation of the process, and not only to evaluate and qualify the product or result.
An autonomous student does not need a teacher to learn	With an autonomous student, it is necessary for the teacher to change his/her role, he/she can guide students' learning process through questions or based his/her own experiences.
	The teacher as an advisor must provide personalized follow-up to the student, at least the same as that used by an algorithm in adaptive learning.
	Adaptive learning lacks the social component, it is desirable that the teacher promotes learning with others.
	The emotional issue, the passion when learning something and the complete experience of the learner are other aspects that the teacher can work on to complement the cognitive and metacognitive dimension.
Project Based Learning generates motivation in students	The affective dimension is very important, the teacher can offer students a learning environment that awakens their interest, fosters a good attitude, disposition, commitment and represents a challenge (achievable).
	The teacher is part of extrinsic motivation, however monitoring, feedback and informing the student about their achievements in their learning process, can promote intrinsic motivation by improving students' self-concept as learners.
	It is important that the teacher inquires with each student about their interests, what excites them and what they need. The teacher should define indicators that allow him/her to recognize whether the student is motivated or not.
	Project-based learning allows students to teach how to establish objectives and goals, this allows the teacher to implement recognition and highlight the feeling of achievement when designing activities and evaluating and providing feedback on the work done by the student

Conclusions

The way of working in the seminar, based on the DDS model, using *Argumente*, has allowed participants to gradually improve their argumentative skills.

The participants, through their work in the seminar, have been identifying the characteristics and abilities of a teacher who encourages autonomy in their students; at the same time, they are building the role of the teacher in the development of autonomous learning

References

Gruendel, K. (2018). The interrelationships between learner autonomy and teacher autonomy. *Relay Journal, 1*(1), 142-146.

Makino, Y. (2009). Logical-narrative thinking revealed: The message construction cross. *The International Journal of Learning, 16*(2), 143-153.

Manrique, L. (2004). El aprendizaje autónomo en la educación a distancia. *Proceedings of the Primer Congreso Virtual Latinoamericano de Educación a Distancia*, 1-11.

Littlewood, W. (1996). Autonomy: An anatomy and a framework. *System, 24*(4), 427-435.

Reinders, H., & Balcikanli, C. (2011). Learning to foster autonomy: The role of teacher education materials. *Studies in Self-Access Learning Journal, 2*(1), 15-25.

Reyes, C., & Moreno, R. (2016). Enseñanza centrada en el estudiante. *ARS MEDICA Revista de Ciencias Médicas, 36*, 107.

Tassinari, M. G. (2012). Evaluating learner autonomy: A dynamic model with descriptors. *Studies in Self-Access Learning Journal, 3*(1), 24-40.

AN ON-LINE TEACHER TRAINING COURSE ON EDUCATION FOR SUSTAINABILITY: ASSESSMENT OF OPEN (MOOC) AND CLOSED VERSIONS OF THE COURSE

Sandra Caeiro, CENSE/FCT/NOVA University of Lisbon and Laboratório de Educação a Distância e ELearning (LE@D), Departamento de Ciências e Tecnologia, Universidade Aberta, João Paz, Laboratório de Educação a Distância e ELearning (LE@D) e Departamento de Educação e Ensino a Distância, Universidade Aberta, Mário Carmo Bastos, Secretaria-Geral da Educação e Ciência, Portugal

Abstract

This paper reports the experience of a first edition of an on-line teacher training course on education for sustainability both for open (MOOC) and closed versions, and the respective assessment. The course was implemented by the Portuguese Distance Learning University (Universidade Aberta – UAb) under a protocol with the General Secretariat of Education and Science of the Portuguese State in an Open EdX platform (NAU). The results show that the planning, preparation of own materials suitable for the target audience and the validation of this type of open/massive and certified closed courses by different actors, before the course taking place is fundamental. It was also confirmed by the positive participation and feedback from the participants. In addition, the collaborative component in both course versions were fundamental to ensure success in this type of training actions. Differences in both versions were discussed as well as recommendations for future editions.

Keywords: Education for sustainable development, MOOC, teachers training, collaborative learning

Introduction

Higher education institutions (HEIs), within the scope of their duties and competencies, and also considering the implementation of the Sustainable Development Goals (SDGs) – Agenda 2030 (UN, 2015), should contribute to ensuring that all students acquire knowledge and skills needed to promote sustainable development, including, among others, through online courses.

In Portugal recent strategies about education for environmental sustainability (e.g. APA, 2016, ME, 2017) recommend the promotion of good practices and projects development in this area in all levels of education. In view of these diverse recommendations and strategies, it is urgent to train and provide trainers, particularly teachers of formal education, with tools so that they can put Sustainability Education into practice in their professional activity. Massive Online Open Courses (MOOCs) have raised remarkable attention throughout the last decade as their initial objective is to provide massive open online education within a collaborative and flexible ways of learning (Teixeira & Mota, 2014).

Earlier experiences have shown that MOOC can have an important role on promoting sustainability literacy (Coelho et al., 2015; Otto et al., 2019). However, in Portugal, full online distance courses were only recently allowed in teachers lifelong training certification and the courses must be closed and have a small number of students with a ratio of 1 teacher/15 students. (CCPFC, 2016).

In this sense, the Portuguese Distance Learning University (UAb) implemented an open (MOOC) and a closed course, for teachers' certification, called Education for Sustainability, developed under a protocol with the General Secretariat of Education and Science of the Portuguese State. The main objective of this paper is thus to report the experience of the first edition of the course (on its open and closed version), by: (a) Presenting the structure and development of the open and closed courses on Education for Sustainability; (b) Justifying the options taken for its development; (c) Analysing the results of student assessment of both open and closed versions of the course; (d) Envisioning improvements for future editions of the course.

Methods

Design of the Course

The aim of this course was to train and provide trainers, in particular teachers of formal education, but not only, with tools to implement Education for Sustainable Development (ESD) projects in their professional activity. The course syllabus was divided into the following 3 topics, each scheduled for 2 weeks, preceded by a boot-camp module (with a workload corresponding to 1.5 European Credits Transfer System, ECTS): Topic 1. Main concepts, policies and strategies; Topic 2. Areas of action in Education for Sustainability; Topic 3. Implementation of Education Projects for Sustainability. The scientific contents followed the recent literature and United Nations recommendations in this thematic area (e.g. Annan-Diab & Molinari, 2017; UNESCO, 2012a; 2012b; 2017).

The courses (MOOC and closed course) were delivered on the NAU platform, the technical publishing infrastructure and course monitoring services for large audiences oriented towards Public Administration and Higher Education (https://lms.nau.edu.pt).

The design and development of the MOOC and closed course went through the following steps:

1. Creation of a Course Guide for each course, composed of the General Objectives, the Specific Contents and Objectives of each Topic, the Learning Environment (the Open EdX platform, used by NAU), the Methodology (based on the Virtual Pedagogical Model of the Open University (Pereira et al., 2007), Resources, Certification (certificate of completion of the course – as long as they performed 2 of the 3 e-activities proposed – or formal accreditation – which required additional work and the payment of a fee, in the case of the MOOC); creation of a video to publicize the course to be hosted on the NAU e-learning platform.
2. Conducting a validation of the objectives, contents and design of the course, through a focus group with a group of specialists and teachers (six in total) in the area and pre-test of the course already implemented on the platform, with two specialists in e-learning. These tests allowed to make several improvements to the course, in terms of content and pedagogy of open/closed, online and massive course teaching.

3. Construction of Resources and implementation of the final version of the course on the NAU platform. Small PDF manuals were developed, and interactive videos were created, with questions embedded through the H5P software and formative and summative activities were built, designed to promote research and critical thinking of the participants (following Leicht et al., 2018). At week 4 a 1-hour synchronous session Webinar was organized with an invited speaker that presented and discussed a success case of ESD implementation at a school. The session was recorded and made available on the course platform.
4. The MOOC and closed course were taught by 2 teachers who accompanied the participants daily for the seven weeks of its duration (from January to March 2020).
5. The course was designed favouring a hybrid approach (Crosslin, 2014), with characteristics of an xMOOC and a cMOOC, in which the participants could choose individual or collaborative e-activities, depending on their preferences or constraints. Participants had available one e-activity by topic (3 in total). E-activities were based on a quiz, sharing of photos and videos of examples of ESD good practices, and reflection about new project themes proposals within ESD. In the case of the MOOC, the e-activities were evaluated by peers, using pre-defined criteria in order to obtain a certificate of participation. In the case of the closed course, the e-activities and a final project assignment was evaluated by the course teachers. For course certificates (in both open and closed) it was mandatory to complete 2 of the 3 e-activities. In the case of the closed course incentives were given for each e-activity successfully achieved (0.5 grades for e-activity). Every week the teachers motivated participants to explore new resources and share and discuss them with the others in the debate forums.
6. To evaluate the course quality, we used the MOOC Quality Checklist developed by the MOOQ project (MOOQ, 2018; Teixeira et al., 2018).

The MOOC was open to any teacher or any participant that wanted to enrol in the course through the NAU platform. In the case of the closed course, the course was first certified by the national body of life long teacher training, and chosen the first 30 (the maximum number allowed for this type of courses) school teachers that registered in the course through UAb registration system.

Course assessment

A pre and post course questionnaire survey was developed aiming, respectively, characterize the participants' profiles and their assessment of the course. The pre-course questionnaire asked about age, education, and motivation for enrolment, previous e-learning and use of open EdX platform experience. The assessment questionnaire was adapted from UAb course assessment questionnaire, used in the institutional UAb MOOCs site (https://aulaberta.uab.pt/). It was developed in Google Forms and delivered to the participants of both courses, respectively at the beginning and end of the courses. The post questionnaire assessed the following dimensions: *Navigation* (5 questions with a 5-Point Likert Scale), *Contents and Activities* (9 questions with a 5-Point Likert Scale), *Interaction and Teaching Support* (2 questions with a 5-Point Likert Scale), *Development of knowledge, skills and attitudes* (4 questions with a 5-Point Likert Scale), *Time Management* (3 questions with a 5-Point Likert Scale), and *Level of Global Satisfaction* (1 question with a 5-Point Likert Scale). Apart from these, there were open response questions about Positive and Negative issues of the course, Suggestions and, if that was the case, reasons for not completing the course. There were some small differences in the questionnaires of the 2 course versions: a question about peer evaluation in the MOOC and a question comparing online with face to face training course experiences in the closed course. Success rates in both courses were calculated and the e-activities collaboration levels and the forums participations were also analysed.

Results and discussion

A total of 702 participants enrolled in the courses, 673 in the MOOC and 29 in the closed course. In the MOOC 136 students successfully completed the course, which corresponds to a 19.5% completion rate. From these 5 participants also requested accreditation. These values were well above the average of the MOOCs completion rates, one of the main criticisms of this type of course (Waks, 2016). In the case of the closed course, 54 % of the participants successfully completed the course, with an average of 8 in 10 for final classification. At the end of the course, the assessment questionnaire obtained a response rate of 20% (141 responses) in the case of the MOOC and 48% (14 responses) in the case of the closed course.

The participants' profile, according to the pre-questionnaire, are presented in Table 1.

Table 1: Course participants' profile

Course	MOOC	Closed course
Age	Between 20-30: 7% Between 31-40: 32% Between 41-50: 36% Between 51-60: 21%	Between 20-30: 16% Between 31-40: 13% Between 41-50: 41% Between 51-60: 25%
Gender	Male: 26% Female: 74%	Male: 14% Female: 86%
Education	Master's degree or above: 70% High school degree or less: 17%	Master's degree or above: >80%
Previous e-learning experience	None: 13% Some: 78%	None: 13% Some: 81%
Previous open EdX platform experience	None: 17% Some: 77%	None: 72% Some: 28%

The participants profiles are rather similar in terms of age and gender distribution (being the closed course participants somewhat older and with more women). In terms of education we find some more latitude in the MOOC, with some high school degree participants. The previous e-learning experience is also very similar but not the previous open EdX platform experience, as most participants in the closed course had no experience and most of the participants of the MOOC had some experience, namely in other NAU courses.

The assessment results show rather positive values in the dimensions Navigation, Contents and Activities, Interaction and Teaching Support, Development of knowledge, skills and attitudes, Time Management and Level of Global Satisfaction (see Table 2, below).

Table 2: Courses' assessment results (dimension averages, scale from 1 to 5)

Dimension	MOOC	Closed course
Navigation	4.13	4.50
Contents and Activities	4.36	4.68
Interaction and Teaching Support	4.12	4.11
Development of knowledge, skills and attitudes	4.46	4.68
Time Management	4.48	4.71
Global Satisfaction	4.43	4.64

The comparison of the 2 courses' global results shows that the closed course participants rated most of the dimensions higher than the MOOC participants. In the case of the *Navigation* dimension, that may be explained by different experience and practice with the Open EdX platform in the 2 groups of participants. The dimension of *Interaction and Teacher Support* was rated in average in a rather similar way in both courses the Teacher Support being rated higher than the Student Interaction level. A component in which the results were still positive, but to a lesser extent was Peer Evaluation (a component of the *Contents and Activities* dimension) in the case of the MOOC, with an average of 3.84. We believe that this was due to a technical problem with the platform, namely, the fact that it did not assign an extension to the file to be transferred and peer evaluated, making it difficult for participants to open it. Even though they were supported (repeatedly) by teachers with instructions on how to proceed to remedy this problem, this had repercussions on the assessment of the peer evaluation process. Regarding the reasons why they did not complete the course, most of the participants mentioned lack of time, namely due to the transition to teleworking, as the COVID-19 pandemic began when the course was taking place. An interesting result, in the closed course, was the average score of 4.14 in the question comparing online to face to face teacher training (the scale ranged from 1-inferior to 5-superior). These results show that it is not only possible to develop online teacher training with quality but also with some advantages over face to face training. That became even more evident a few months later with a surge in the online teacher training offers due to the COVID-19 pandemic.

Although collaborative e-activities were encouraged, only about 10% of the participants, in both courses, choose to work in group. One reason that may explain these results is the fact that online group work and coordination is more demanding than doing the assignments individually. Non-mandatory interaction in the forums (sharing of resources and initiatives) were proportionally higher in the open course. In the certified and closed course participants seemed to be more focused on the mandatory and graded tasks.

With the balance of the course completed, the aspects to be improved are mainly of a technical nature associated with the platform: ensuring better functioning of the peer evaluation, resolve the issue of the platform not sending a copy of messages from the forums to email, which allows for better teacher monitoring, and the fact that participants are unable to attach files to forum messages, which limits collaborative work. In addition, some changes in the schedule of activities will also be considered and will be implemented in a 2nd edition of the course. Bearing in mind collaborative and team advantages for the e-learning process (Teixeira & Mota, 2014) and in particular considering the holistic and integrated approach of ESD (Annan-Diab & Molinari, 2017; UNESCO, 2012b; 2017) we will try to rethink their design, support tools and evaluation so that more participants will choose collaborative e-activities. Incentives, like badges, could be used in this context, as they can foster learning engagement and creativity (Bidarra & Rusman, 2017).

Conclusions

It can be concluded that the planning, preparation of own materials suitable for the target audience, the validation of this type of open/massive and certified closed courses by different actors and the collaborative component and exchange of experiences, were fundamental to ensure success of the training actions. HEIs with their experience and knowledge thus have a fundamental role in the implementation of these courses and can contribute to teach wider audiences, outside the formal educational system, on topics as necessary as those related to the Sustainable Development Goals. Both open and closes courses had high level of satisfaction, highlighting that MOOCs can be a learning tool useful for teacher training.

References

Annan-Diab, F., & Molinari, C. (2017). Interdisciplinarity: Practical approach to advancing education for sustainability and for the Sustainable Development Goals. *The International Journal of Management Education, 15*, 73-83.

APA. (2016). *Caminho para uma Estratégia Nacional de Educação Ambiental 2020.* Agência Portuguesa do Ambiente.

Bidarra, J. E., & Rusman, E. (2017) Towards a pedagogical model for science education: bridging educational contexts through a blended learning approach. *Open Learning: The Journal of Open, Distance and e-Learning, 32*(1), 6-20.

CCPFC. (2016). *Regulamento para acreditação e creditação de acções de formação contínua.* Conselho Científico-Pedagógico da Formação Contínua.

Coelho, J., Teixeira, A., Caeiro, S., Nicolau, P., & Rocio, V. (2015). iMOOC on Climate Change: Evaluation of a Massive Open Online Learning Pilot Experience. *International Review of Research in Open and Distributed Learning, 16*(6). 152-173.

Crosslin, M. (2014, May 4). Designing a Dual Layer cMOOC/xMOOC. EduGeek Journal [Blog post]. Retrieved from https://www.edugeekjournal.com/2014/05/04/designing-a-dual-layer-cmoocxmooc/

Leicht, A., Combes, B., Byun, W., & Agbedahin, A. (2018). From Agenda 21 to Target 4.7: the development of Education for Sustainable Development. In A. Leicht, J. Heiss, & W. Byun (Eds.), *Issues and trends in Education for Sustainable Development* (1st ed., pp. 25-38). Paris: United Nations Educational, Scientific and Cultural Organization (UNESCO).

ME. (2017). *Referencial de Educação Ambiental para a Sustentabilidade. Ministério da Educação.* Direção Geral da Educação. Retrieved from http://www.dge.mec.pt/sites/default/files/ECidadania/Educacao_Ambiental/documentos/reas_cons ulta_publica.pdf

MOOQ. (2018). MOOQ for the Quality of MOOCs. Retrieved from http://mooc-quality.eu/

Otto, D. Caeiro, S., Nioclua, P. Disterhelft, A., Teixeira, A., Becker, S., Bollmann, A., & Sander, K. (2019). Can MOOCs empower people to critically think about climate change? A learning outcome based comparison of two MOOCs. *Journal of Cleaner Production, 222*, 12-21.

Teixeira, A., & Mota, J. (2014). A proposal for the methodological design of collaborative language MOOCs. In E. Martín-Monje & E. Barcena (Eds.), *Language MOOCs: Providing Learning, Transcending Boundaries*. DE GRUYTER OPEN.

Teixeira, A., Stracke, C., Pinto, M. do C., & Paz, J. (2018, April). *Building a Common Quality Reference Framework for Improving, Assessing and Comparing MOOC Design.* Paper presented at the MOOCMaker Global Symposium. Retrieved from https://core.ac.uk/download/pdf/158844207.pdf

Pereira, A., Quintas-Mendes, A., Morgado, L., Amante, L., & Bidarra, J. (2007). *Modelo pedagógico virtual da Universidade Aberta: para uma universidade do futuro.* Universidade Aberta.

Waks, L. J. (2016). *The Evolution and Evaluation of Massive Open Online Courses.* Palgrave Macmillan US. https://doi.org/10.1057/978-1-349-85204-8

United Nations. (2015). *Sustainable Development Goals.* Retrieved June 30, 2020, from https://nacoesunidas.org/conheca-os-novos-17-objetivos-de-desenvolvimento-sustentavel-da-onu/

UNESCO (2012a). *Shaping the Education of Tomorrow 2012.* Report on the UN Decade of Education for Sustainable Development, Abridged. DESD Monitoring and Evaluation. ISBN 978-92-3-001076-8.

UNESCO (2012b). *Education for Sustainable Development.* Source Book. UNESCO. ISBN 978-92-3001063-8.

UNESCO (2017). *Education for Sustainable Development Goals. Learning Objectives.* Education 2030. United Nations Educational, Scientific and Cultural Organization. France. ISBN 978-92-3-100209-0.

THE POTENTIAL OF USING SMARTPHONE IN TEACHING AND LEARNING IN SECONDARY SCHOOL – A DESCRIPTIVE STUDY OF SELECTED SCHOOLS IN MAPUTO CITY

Mphatso Imwa, Pedro Cabral, Laboratory of Distance Education & eLearning, Universidade Aberta, Portugal

Introduction

Today, the Smartphone has become one of the most potent and vital devices in the educational field. With its capability to connect to the Internet and provide people with access to millions of websites, and access to a variety of both commercial and non-commercial, online and offline apps from Android and iOS platforms which accounts to over 4.4 million (Clement, 2020), makes it an ideal substitute for a physical library or physical classroom. Ozdamli (2012), claims that with the developments of mobile technologies such as smartphones, education is under transformation towards more learner-centric theories, i.e., constructivist, situated, collaborative, informal, and lifelong learning. Herrington and Herrington (2007), further argue that justifiable conditions exist that mobile technologies provide a medium for authentic learning (p.1). Smartphone apps such as telegram, WhatsApp, Facebook, and YouTube give the students ability to connect with different experts from different fields of learning while in their hospital beds, from the comfort of their own homes, and convenient zones, on the go, and from diverse time zones and geographical positions with ease. Peters (2005), argues that mobile technologies provide a "just enough," "just in time," and "just for me" model of flexible learning (p.3). This implies that students are free to choose what they want/need to learn without being forced to participate in a class, which deems necessary for them.

The smartphone features and applications like photo/video/sound shooting, and its storage capacity gives it a tremendous educational value in promoting social, interactive, and collaborative learning. Students can store and retrieve, create, and share new knowledge, curiosity, findings, and reports through different multimedia modes. Also, since smartphones promote mobile learning, learning, therefore, becomes spontaneous, continuous, lifelong and informal as students do not need to be in physical schools or classrooms necessarily; instead, it is ubiquitous.

In different disciplines, such as Science and language education, smartphones have a significant role in improving and increasing the speed at which the learners may learn a new language. The applications such as Google Translate help students to learn a new language instantly and effectively, hence, its ability to provide not only the translation but also the synonyms and correct audio pronunciation of the words in different languages. Apps such as Hello Pal, Babbel, and Duolingo have created a massive community of language students who wish to learn languages other than their mother tongues. Students can interact and learn exchange-ably with speakers from different language backgrounds. Math games, Khan Academy, and Grasshopper provide students with updated content, competitions and tests which help them acquire new knowledge, or cover the knowledge gap missed during classes at school. The Smartphone may help students to learn things ahead of their formal curriculum and stages, therefore allowing all categories of learners, i.e., fast average and slow, to learn at their own pace and finish the curriculum content with ease.

As smartphone ownership and use increase, thanks to affordability, connectivity, and internet expansion globally, it is no longer surprising to see both teachers and students owning a mobile or Smartphone even in developing countries such as Mozambique. Such penetration of mobile devices among the people is valuable in the implementation and delivery of education in this time when institutions, educators, and scholars are shifting to forms of social learning such as mobile, online, and e-learning. In the developing world like Mozambique, embracing mobile technologies such as a smartphone is paramount to improving the quality and quantity of teaching and learning.

The need to cope with the advancements in information and communication technology and transition to more learner-centred education, where the learners construct the knowledge than being transmitted to (Hamdan, 2014), the government of Mozambique through its ministry of education launched its educational, technological plan in 2011. The proposal recommended a shift from traditional (pedagogy of transmission) to the constructivist model, which supports interaction and collaboration in learning (MINED, 2011). Such a model encourages learners to create content and share it among them and regard teachers as one who map the way for learners to discover knowledge, "a facilitator," "coaches," and "co-learner" (S. Al Hamdani 2014; p.42). The PTE outlined the supplying of computers in schools where both teachers and students can have access to virtual learning environments and digital learning materials and learn interactively with both teachers, specialists, and even at home. While the plan is realistic in this digital era, it is also challenging to implement it for a developing country, in this case, Mozambique. Computers are still expensive to purchase for all schools nationwide. However, considering the proliferation, ubiquity, and affordability of smartphones, perhaps an alternative is just a step away. According to O'Dea (2020b), the year 2020 has over 3.5 billion smartphone users worldwide (see graph 1.1). In 2018, Mozambique, with a population of at least 30 million ("Mozambique Population (2020) – Worldometer", 2020), has at least 14 million mobile phone subscriptions (O'Dea, 2020a), which includes over 6.5 million internet users as of the year 2020. The figures demonstrate excellent development in access to data in general. From the educational perspective, it is specifically a milestone as the presence of smartphones provides essential features and uses, which can improve secondary school education in Mozambique. But to establish concrete theories or practical principles around the use of smartphones in teaching and learning in the context of Mozambique, it is crucial to explore the features, uses, perceptions and challenges around its use among the teachers and students.

Research objectives

This article is a product of a research headlined above. Its main objective was to explore the potential use of smartphone in teaching and learning in secondary schools in Maputo province of Mozambique. Specifically, the study aimed at identifying the potential features that smartphones have in education; assessing the perceptions that teachers and students have towards smartphone use in teaching and learning and exploring the challenges that surround its use in secondary school education. The aims derived from the observation that smartphone proliferation is increasing rapidly in developing countries, that both students and teachers have access to the mobile devices, therefore overlooking its presence undermines the potential that smartphone has in teaching and learning in secondary schools.

Methodology

Method and sample population

This study deployed a descriptive method which answers the question "what" instead of "how" and "why something has happened" (Nassaji, 2015; p.129) or "why reality is showing itself this way" (Lans & van der Voordt, 2002; p.53). Loeb et al. (2017) also argues that descriptive research is concerned with the study of "realworld needs, which can warrant policy and intervention" (p.2). In other ways, researchers study the phenomena under peoples' perceptions.

In the context of this study, a sample of 18 teachers and 55 students of grade 11 and 12 from the selected schools respectively voluntarily agreed to participate. The process was through a non-probabilistic sampling technic which do not oblige the researcher to single out specific individuals.

Table 1: Gender characteristics of the respondents

	Males	Females	Total
Teachers	8	10	18
Students	28	27	55
Total	36	37	73

Questionnaires and procedure

Two questionnaires were created, one for the students and the other for the teacher participants. Prior to deploying the questionnaires, a pilot study was conducted to help correct the problems such as language errors, clarity, simplicity of language and research protocols (such as participant informed consent) and determine how much time one may need to fill out the questionnaire. Once the issues were resolved, the researcher distributed the questionnaires to 60 students and 30 teachers respectively. 55 students returned them filled which represent a 93.3 percent. 18 teachers returned the questionnaires representing a 60 percent response rate. On average, there was a 77 percent response rate from teachers and students.

The data collection was anonymous, therefore, demanded participants not to reveal their identity but only their age range which was 16 and above. Having the two questionnaires made it possible for the groups to speak for itself other than the other. The questions in the survey tools were mostly closed-ended, demanding the respondent's level of agreement through a five-level Likert scale between strongly agree and strongly disagree. In some questions, respondents needed to select their best answer.

Results

General background of the politics of ICT in education at the study schools

It was essential to discover if the school has any transparent ICT policy and if all teachers are aware of it. The discovery would reveal the extent to which the school promotes the use of any ICT at its disposal to assist in improving the quality teaching and learning. Teachers had to choose; *Yes*, *No*, or *I do not know*, from the pre-inserted responses. Those who responded *yes* would later explain the policy in writing. The results (see Table 2) show that majority (12) of teachers confirmed the existence of the ICT policy in the schools. Only two teachers responded *no* to the question, and the remaining four showed they do not know of the school's ICT policy.

Table 2: School's policy on ICT in teaching and learning

	Yes	No	I don't know	TOTAL
Frequency	12	2	4	18

The table above demonstrates the lack of unison response which entails possible lack of schools' own policy over ICT in education. However, when asked whether the schools promote the use of ICT in teaching and learning, despite not having a clear ICT policy. Interestingly all 18 teachers responded positively to the question demonstrating their awareness of the potential of ICT in improving teaching and learning. Teachers further mentioned the presence of devices such as thin clients, cellphones, television and projectors which they do use in some cases. The study also revealed that 13 (72%) teachers had had training in technology use, and only five (28%) did not have (see graph 4).

Potential uses of the Smartphone in teaching and learning

Under this item, nine statements supporting the use of smartphones in the teaching and learning process were made. They include; enabling seamless way of learning anywhere and at any time, continuous engagement and interaction with students sending short texts, images, and videos to students, access to vast educational apps and resources from the internet among others. The last statement was about confirming whether some teachers have never thought of using the device in teaching and learning process. In general, more than 80 percent of the teachers on average agreed to the statements, and interestingly 51 percent made strong affirmations implying that they do know the potential the smartphones have in education. Eleven percent of the teachers remained neutral, and another 6 percent agreed to the statement that they never thought of smartphone as a pedagogical tool, which may imply to the outcome of some neutral or non-affirmative responses to the first 9 statements.

Perception about the use of smartphones in secondary school among teachers and students

Eighteen statements around perceptions of teachers towards smartphone use in teaching process were created. 10 deemed the devices as positive learning tools offering personalized learning environment, promoting collaboration, engaging timid learners, extending physical class to cyber-class and promoting social learning among others. The other 8 statements positioned the smartphone as inappropriate learning device which among other reasons promote distraction where students spend more time socializing instead of learning, promoting only entertainment and sharing illicit content. The results have shown that at least 70 percent of teachers deem the smartphone as a learning device by responding affirmatively to the first 10 statements. Another 40 percent of teachers disagreed to viewing smartphones as distraction tools. However, the results also showed that teachers understand the challenges that students may use smartphones to share illicit content and spending more time on activities other than learning.

On the other hand, when students were asked about their perceptions towards smartphone use in learning, 49 students agreed that a smartphone is a vital tool for learning. Five students disagreed, and one student stood undecided. On whether the smartphone is relevant for leisure or not, 45, in general, agreed. In contrast, six neither agreed nor disagreed, and four disagreed. The results paint a picture that students are aware of the importance of the device in their learning adventures in addition to using it as an entertainment tool. See Table 3

Table 3: Is the smartphone an essential tool in your learning?

Q3	Statement	Strongly Agree	Agree	Neither Agree/ Disagree	Disagree	Strongly Disagree
3A	O Smartphone é uma ferramenta significativa para a minha aprendizagem	27 (49%)	22 (40%)	1 (2%)	5 (9%)	0 (0%)
3B	Os smartphones são relevantes para o meu tempo de lazer ou entretenimento	12 (22%)	33 (60%)	6 (11%)	4 (7%)	0 (0%)

Students were further asked to rank the top 5 activities from the list of 14 which they deem important in their daily use of smartphone, WhatsApp, dictionary Duolingo YouTube and internet surfing were the platforms selected most. The results were similar to that of teachers except that text translator and reading books/news/audiobooks ranked 1 and 3 respectively.

Both teachers and students were also asked to choose disciplines they think smartphone are well aligned. The results came out that Language and scientific subjects ranked first and send compared to arts, and humanity subjects respectively.

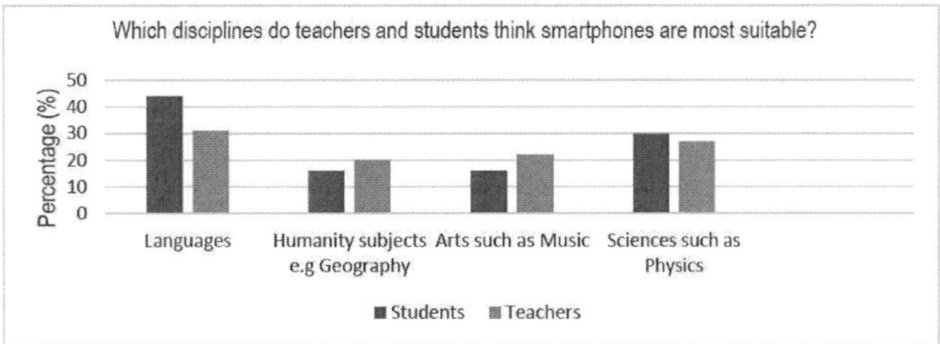

Graph 1. Suitability of smartphone in subject

Challenges around the use of smartphones in secondary schools

The objective behind the item was to discover what teachers consider to be the barriers, problems, and challenges around the use or adoption of smartphones in teaching and learning in secondary school. Under this question, 11 statements were created based on what the review of literature narrated. The statements included whether the cost is a challenge, the ease of use, connectivity, and flooding of information, among others. Overall, at least 50 percent of the respondents concurred to the challenges. Seventeen (17) teachers who represent 84 percent agreed that lack of technical knowledge among them is the greatest challenge. Second is the incompatibility of some applications and the cost of some useful apps (84%), and thirdly, the higher cost of the internet (83%). Fifty percent of teachers disagreed on the point that there is a lack of learning content in context and according to the geographic reality, and six teachers (33%) remained undecided at the same point. Twelve teachers (67%) disagreed with the statement that smartphones are difficult to use in learning situations. Another 67 percent also disagreed that it is difficult to find information on the internet using smartphones. Results are distributed equally on whether students may stop learning due to mass information such as through social platforms like Facebook and WhatsApp.

Conclusion

This study traversed the characteristics, uses, perceptions, and challenges which circumambient smartphone use in secondary school education among teachers and students. The survey findings demonstrate the awareness among teachers and students that smartphone is and can impact positive teaching and learning processes. However not it is evident from the findings that not all features and functions of smartphones are in use, or perhaps have been fully exploited to benefit teaching and learning. Such features include photo/video camera, playing games, and other specific educational applications such as Khan Academy. WhatsApp and Facebook are found to be highly used. Unless specific activities and concrete evidence are presented, the study cannot confidently prove that what students do with the said apps is educational. By considering the time frame and human resources, limitations such as sample size were considered, and therefore it can be problematic to generalize the results. Overall, the findings should provide an inspiration window into similar or further investigation of issues such as;

- There is a need for much more extensive research of the similar nature in Mozambique. An investigation that can involve teachers and students from remote areas, urban, and cities to check and compare the differences in attitudes towards incorporating mobile devices as pedagogical tools in classrooms.
- A rigorous capacity training for teachers on how they can use smartphones and other mobile devices as useful pedagogical tools in classrooms is highly essential; hence undermining the presence of the devices among students can compromise students' performance.
- The study recommends a Digital literacy campaign among students as it would help students effectively use smartphones in their education on top of daily communication. It can be expected that a literate student population will entirely be responsible and therefore reducing the malpractices such as sharing of illicit or unnecessary content
- A practical study on student engagement in online learning platforms to see how shy or timid learners participate in learning activities will help establish specific methods or techniques which can yield maximum participation results.
- The study further recommends an action type of research which tries out some specific smartphone applications in particular discipline or subjects and compare the performance of students taught without a mobile device. Such an inquiry would help project the level of motivation and engagement of students in different learning activities when mobile devices such as a smartphone are in use.

References

Clement, J. (2020, September 01). Number of apps in leading app stores. Retrieved March 2, 2020, from https://www.statista.com/statistics/276623/number-of-apps-available-in-leading-app-stores/

Herrington, A., & Herrington, J. (2007). Authentic mobile learning in higher education. *Proceedings of the Australian Association for Research in Education (AARE) 2007 Conference,* 1-9. Fremantle. Retrieved from http://www.aare.edu.au/07pap/her07131.pdf

Lans, W., & van der Voordt, T. (2002). *Ways to study – Descriptive research.*

Loeb, S., Dynarski, S., McFarland, D., Morris, P., Reardon, S., & Reber, S. (2017). *Descriptive analysis in education: A guide for researchers.* (NCEE 2017–4023).

Washington, DC: U.S. Department of Education, Institute of Education Sciences, National Center for Education Evaluation and Regional Assistance.

Minestério de Educação (MINED) - Governo de Moçambique. (2011). 2011 Plano Tecnológico da Educação [PDF]. MINED

Mozambique Population (2020) - Worldometer. (2020). Retrieved 7 May 2020, from https://www.worldometers.info/worldpopulation/mozambique-population/

Nassaji, H. (2015). Qualitative and descriptive research: Data type versus data analysis. *Language Teaching Research, 19*(2), 129–132. doi:10.1177/1362168815572747

O'Dea, S. (2020a). Mozambique mobile cellular subscriptions 2000-2018 | Statista. Retrieved 5 May 2020, from https://www.statista.com/statistics/500997/number-of-mobile-cellular-subscriptions-in-mozambique/

O'Dea, S. (2020b). Smartphone users worldwide 2020 | Statista. Retrieved 5 May 2020, from https://www.statista.com/statistics/330695/number-of-smartphone-users-worldwide/

Ozdamli, F. (2012). Pedagogical framework of m-learning. *Social and behavioral Sciences 31*(2011), 927–931. https://doi.org/10.1016/j.sbspro.2011.12.171

Peters, K. (2005, January 1). Learning on the move: Mobile technologies in business and education. Canberra: Commonwealth of Australia

S. Al Hamdani, D. (2014). A Constructivist Approach to a Mobile Learning Environment. *International Journal of Computer Applications, 93*(4), 41-46. doi:10.5120/16206-5500

RESEARCH NETWORKING IN A DIGITAL WORLD: THE CASE OF COSTA RICA'S UNED RESEARCH NETWORK ON DISTANCE, ONLINE AND OPEN EDUCATION, REDIC

Maynor Barrientos, Universidad Estatal a Distancia Costa Rica, Costa Rica

Abstract

This presentation reviews the principles, structure, methodology and major achievements of the International Research Network on Distance, Online and Open Education (REDIC) led by the Costa Rica's State University of Distance Education since 2017. REDIC is a research network based on dynamic relationships between actors, agents, individuals, and organizations. Its main objective is to generate a space for academic and research relationships characterized by ties, common areas of research, collaborative scientific publication and a portfolio of internationally-funded projects. REDIC has members from more than 25 countries around the world. REDIC has been UNED's Research Program in Foundations of Distance Education most important strategy to cope with its adaptation to the digital world of research through activities, strategies and products that have exploited the advantages of today's digital technological growth and diversification.

Keywords: Research Networks; Digital Learning; Distance and Online Education; International Cooperation

Introduction

Higher education institutions all around the world have been transitioning toward digital organizations mainly forced by the transformation of the educational industry into Education 4.0 and Industry 4.0 business models (Bond, Marín, Dolch, Bedenlier, & Zawacki-Richter, 2018; Fischer, Komlosi, Baracskai, & Baracskai, 2020). Most recent research in relation to higher education institutional modernization has concentrated on the changes, challenges, advances, and obstacles related to the services and technological innovations affecting the processes of teaching and learning in the digital university ecosystems (Kwet & Prinsloo, 2020; Valks, Arkesteijn, Koutamanis, & den Heijer, 2020). Less has been explored about those challenges related to research in distance, online or hybrid higher education institutions (Teixeira, Bates, & Mota, 2019).

Research units have also been challenged by the rapid digital transformation of higher education institutions, and they have become dependent upon their ability to form academic and research networks that work well in the current digital world (Oliveira & Morgado, 2018; Aithal, & Aithal, 2019; 2020).

Those regions and countries better prepared for the 21st century Industry 4.0 revolution have responded in a better way when adjusting their public and private sectors to adapt and respond to challenges and obstacles. Higher education institutions in those regions have, therefore, been better prepared to adjust their research activities and units cope with their digital transformations and establishment of online research networks (van Galen, 2019; Crow & Dabars, 2020). However, for other regions (Zawacki-Richter & Qayyum, 2019), such as Central America and the Caribbean, HEIs have had more difficulties in adjusting the digital organizational modes in terms of teaching process and more so in terms of research processes.

In Central America, Costa Rica's State University of Distance Education has been a pioneering HEI in its educational model, with more than 40 years of experience in distance education and more than 20 years in online teaching and learning. In that sense, UNED's institutional model has adjusted well to technological change and to specific economic, social and health crises like the one provoked by COVID-19. In terms of research, UNED's research system was constituted as recently as 2007, with the creation of its Research Department and the creation of several research units (Amador, 2014)

Among those research units, UNED's Research Program in Foundations of Distance Education (PROIFED) has been conducting research projects on several topics all related to UNED's educational and institutional models and has been addressing the challenges posed by the current tendencies of online research processes and activities. Among PROIFED's main strategies in adapting to the digital world of research has been the establishment of an international research network which has exploited the advantages of today's digital technological growth and diversification activities, strategies and products.(Cascante-Gatgens, 2020; 2021).

This presentation will provide an overview of the International Research Network on Distance, Online and Open Education (REDIC), its main agenda, research lines, strategies and academic and research products and results after two years of work. REDIC aims at becoming an international hub that can bring together research opportunities and exchange of experiences of research groups from all over the world.

Background

REDIC is promoted by the Research Program in Foundations of Distance Education (PROIFED) of Costa Rica's State University of Distance Education (UNED), universities, research centres, national and international researchers, students, and enthusiasts around the world.

REDIC arises as part of PROIFED's strategic planning process. The preparation of the PROIFED strategic plan (2018-2023), was itself the result of the project "Management Model for the Research Program of Fundamentals in Distance Education (PROIFED) of Costa Rica's State University of Distance Education (UNED): A proposal based on the approach of Organizations Open to Learning and Strategic Thinking" that started in 2015 (Mora, Meneses, & Barrientos, 2018).

As a research unit, PROIFED's main purpose is to generate knowledge in the field of Distance Education, knowledge that can be transferred and at the same time implemented within UNED and through its national and international links.

REDIC has adopted PROIFED's main strategy to develop its international agenda and to strengthen its international cooperation possibilities.

REDIC Academic Networking Principles

REDIC is based on the basic principles of collaborative work in academia (academic networks) through which benefits are obtained by all members, especially in terms of discovery, integration, application of knowledge and learning (Jordan, 2019; Weller, 2011).

The network is founded on the basis of dynamic relationships between actors, agents, individuals or organizations; that is, a set of exchange actions, compromises, traffic or bonds established between two or more entities; these actions can be definable, observable, representable and traceable (Easley & Kleinberg, 2012). In another sense, the network is the specific space that is formed as a result of the existence of this set of relationships between the partners and the space that is "naturally" delimited according to the size and scope of the interaction (Barthelemy, 2011).

From these perspectives, the network is formed around three fundamental definitions:

1. The specification of the members and stakeholders connected inside.
2. The nature of the type of interactions established between the members.
3. The topological relationship that is involved in its formation and growth.

Even though there are already a significant number of groups in the world concerned with distance education, virtual education or open education (Zawacki-Richter & Naidu, 2016; Bond, Zawacki-Richter, & Nichols, 2019), REDIC is the first of its kind, since it is based on the logic of integration of social networks, and seeks to build a bridge between the experiences and developments of distance, online and open educational researches from all continents, schools and trends, between public, private and academic sectors, focusing on academic exchange and less on internal administration or management (Salmi, 2017).

This is especially relevant for Central America and the Caribbean, a region where virtual or distance education experiences have not been adequately systematized, nor where detailed studies have been made on the needs of national or institutional educational systems that can prepare Central American countries for the future of digital learning, education 4.0, the adoption of technologies that have transformed education and pedagogical sciences in this century (Gilligan, 2020).

Objective

REDIC's main objective is to generate a space for academic and research relationships characterized by ties, common areas of research, collaborative scientific publication and a portfolio of internationally-funded projects through a defined set of multi-level interactions between the members of the network.

Structure

REDIC has a horizontal collaboration structure formed by individual, institutional nodes and other networks of researchers, managers, and academics with experience in distance, online or open education. It is also made up of international experts, professors, teachers, students and enthusiasts of distance and online education.

Its organization and orientation are headed by a group of leaders, based on the certainty of the potentialities of well-defined relationships between the members, actors, and agents of REDIC.

More than on a well constituted regulatory framework, REDIC's strength lies in the benefit that its members find in the synergy that the group and group members create.

The success of the network, therefore, is the value of its interactions, achievements, and the strength of its digital space of development. This functioning is supported by network behaviour analysis that focus more on the exchange flows within a network (and how these flows are motivated) than on the *a priori* structural conditions that have promoted the conception of a possible network (Borgatti, 2005). In this sense the network derives its strength less from the nodes of the network than from the relationships between the nodes.

The members of the REDIC add value to the network with their participation and with their relationships in different projects, developments and products achieved with other nodes. Members must be well characterized and engage efficiently (Waheed, Klobas, & Ain, 2020). To establish objectives for the network beyond those referred to exchange and value-added relationships among its members, the specific interests of each individual member or institution participating in REDIC are weighed. Thus, the REDIC network starts from a clear idea of relationship, interaction and joint work, each member gaining value for belonging to the network and, therefore, other collaboration objectives are shared.

Methodology

The REDIC methodology of work derives from the following questions: What are the essential types of relationships between network members? How are essential relationships defined? How is the existence of these relationships verified, represented, and tracked or recorded? Are these one-way or reciprocal relationships? What other relationships will stem from these essential initial dynamics, and how can they be verified, represented, tracked, or recorded? What topological, physical, or geo-referential expectations should be considered over time as the network grows? (Barão, de Vasconcelos, Rocha, & Pereira, 2017; Crawley, Hegarty, Edström, & Sanchez, 2020).

Thus, REDIC has established the following methodological scheme:

1. Characterization of agents according to a matrix of interest of all possible members of the network.
2. Establishment of a series of possible relationships between these members, according to their interests and material possibilities; will the members of this network be able to...? Are there minimum conditions for these relationships between members of the network to be possible?
3. Establishment of a minimum policy and regulatory framework specifically focused on relationships and basic interests established by the network, and according to the actual material conditions for interactions between the members.
4. A hierarchy of network objectives in accordance with basic relationships and setting of short- and medium-term objectives with a guarantee of immediate materiality according to the conditions of possibility of effective relationships.
5. Establishment of the initial spatial limits for the network and the methods of monitoring and tracking spatial growth through specialized software for the digital representation of networks.

6. Emphasis on the elementary conditions to initiate exchange relationships between the members of the network, through strategies, activities, and initial co-investments, rather than on a priori regulatory, management or "governance" aspects.
7. Careful establishment of long-term objectives for the network, on material basis and realistic resources and according to the potentialities derived from the relationships of the network and the added value of its members.
8. Growth of the network and its spatial scope over time and on data derived from its actions and not according to predetermined political or legal frameworks.

REDIC Research areas

International Cooperation in Distance and Online Education; Open Educational Resources; Educational Technology for Distance and Online Education Models; Innovative Institutional Organization Models; Educational Innovation; New Services for Students; Quality Systems for Distance and Online Education; Innovative Pedagogy for Distance and Online Education; Ethics, Democratization and Social Inclusion in Distance and Online Education; Academic Mobility, Collaborative International Publication and International Research Portfolios.

Members

REDIC is made up of more than 120 researchers of institutions from Argentina, Brazil, Canada, China, Costa Rica, Colombia, Cuba, El Salvador, Scotland, Spain, United States, Guatemala, Holland, Honduras, Japan, Mexico, Nicaragua, New Zealand, Panama, Peru, Portugal, Puerto Rico, United Kingdom, Dominican Republic, South Africa, and Venezuela.

Main Achievements

Among REDIC major achievements (since 2017?) are more than 30 online international academic activities, more than 20 international academic exchanges, the publication of 9 books with international cooperation by more than 15 researchers from 6 different countries, 5 international research projects, and the establishment of different international agreements and internetwork connections.

Future Agenda

REDIC in coordination with different associated networks, and members universities and organization, will be holding the I Online Summit on Education, Research and Digital Technologies in March 25-27, 2021. This summit consists of three major events: the II REDIC International Meeting, 2021; the II International Meeting of Interuniversity Student Research; and the II Summit of Digital Education.

References

Aithal, P. S., & Aithal, S. (2019). Strategic Management of Universal Technologies for Redefining Productivity & Performance. *International Journal of Applied Engineering and Management Letters (IJAEML), 3*(2), 81-95.

Aithal, P. S., & Aithal, S. (2020). Promoting Faculty and Student Centered Research and Innovation based Excellence Model to Reimage Universities. *International Journal of Management, Technology, and Social Sciences (IJMTS), 5*(1), 24-41.

Amador, M. B. (2014). La administración de la investigación en la Universidad Estatal a Distancia de Costa Rica: revisión histórica desde 1977 hasta 2006. *Revista Espiga, 28*, 61-73.

Barão, A., de Vasconcelos, J. B., Rocha, Á., & Pereira, R. (2017). A knowledge management approach to capture organizational learning networks. *International Journal of Information Management, 37*(6), 735-740.

Borgatti, S. P. (2005). Centrality and network flow. *Social Networks, 27*(1), 55-71.

Barthélemy, M. (2011). Spatial networks. *Physics Reports, 499*(1-3), 1-101.

Bond, M., Zawacki-Richter, O., & Nichols, M. (2019). Revisiting five decades of educational technology research: A content and authorship analysis of the British Journal of Educational Technology. *British Journal of Educational Technology, 50*(1), 12-63.

Bond, M., Marín, V. I., Dolch, C., Bedenlier, S., & Zawacki-Richter, O. (2018). Digital transformation in German higher education: student and teacher perceptions and usage of digital media. *International Journal of Educational Technology in Higher Education, 15*(1), 48.

Cascante-Gatgens, A. (2020). La investigación como promotora de la innovación y la vinculación social: el caso del PROIFED de la Universidad Estatal a Distancia de Costa Rica. *Revista Latinoamericana de Educación y Estudios Interculturales, 4*(3).

Cascante-Gatgens, A. (2021). Estrategias de internacionalización de unidades de investigación en las universidades públicas: El caso del PROIFED de la UNED de Costa Rica. *Revista Panorama, 15*(28).

Casciaro, T., & Lobo, M. S. (2005). Competent jerks, lovable fools, and the formation of social networks. *Harvard Business Review, 83*(6), 92-99.

Crawley, E., Hegarty, J., Edström, K., & Sanchez, J. C. G. (2020). Supporting the Academic Mission of the Adaptable University. In E. Crawley, J. Hegarty, K. Edström, & J. C. G. Sanchez (Eds.), *Universities as Engines of Economic Development* (pp. 201-238). Springer, Cham.

Crow, M. M., & Dabars, W. B. (2020). *The Fifth Wave: The Evolution of American Higher Education.* Johns Hopkins University Press.

Easley, D., & Kleinberg, J. (2012). Networks, crowds, and markets: Reasoning about a highly connected world. *Significance, 9*, 43-44.

Fischer, P., Komlosi, L. I., Baracskai, S., & Baracskai, Z. (2020). Smart Education for The Digital Era-Why We Need to Abandon Traditional Learning Styles and Let Digital Natives Do What They Do Best. *Economic and Social Development (Book of Proceedings), 52nd International Scientific Conference on Economic and Social Development*, 185.

van Galen, S. (2019). *Shaping European universities.* Routledge.

Gilligan, J. (2020). Competencies for Educators in Delivering Digital Accessibility in Higher Education. *Proceedings of the International Conference on Human-Computer Interaction*, 184-199. Springer, Cham.

Gulati, R. (1999). Network location and learning: The influence of network resources and firm capabilities on alliance formation. *Strategic Management Journal, 20*(5), 397-420.

Jordan, K. (2019). From social networks to publishing platforms: a review of the history and scholarship of academic social network sites. *Frontiers in Digital Humanities, 6*, 5.

Kwet, M., & Prinsloo, P. (2020). The 'smart' classroom: a new frontier in the age of the smart university. *Teaching in Higher Education, 25*(4), 510-526.

Mora Umaña, A. M., Meneses Hernández, J., & Barrientos Amador, M. (Eds.). (2018). *Escenarios de la investigación en educación a distancia.* San José, Costa Rica: Universidad Estatal a Distancia.

Oliveira, N. R., & Morgado, L. (2018). Digital Identity of Researchers 2.0: The Case of Their Personal Learning Network. In *Information Retrieval and Management: Concepts, Methodologies, Tools, and Applications* (pp. 2063-2082). IGI Global.

Salmi, J. (2017). The Changing Context: New Challenges, New Opportunities. In J. Salmi (Ed.), *The Tertiary Education Imperative* (pp. 1-30). Brill Sense.

Smith, D. A., & Lohrke, F. T. (2008). Entrepreneurial network development: Trusting in the process. *Journal of Business Research, 61*(4), 315-322.

Teixeira, A. M., Bates, T., & Mota, J. (2019). What future (s) for distance education universities? Towards an open network-based approach. *RIED: Revista Iberoamericana de Educación a Distancia, 22*(1), 107236.

Valks, B., Arkesteijn, M. H., Koutamanis, A., & den Heijer, A. C. (2020). Towards a smart campus: supporting campus decisions with Internet of Things applications. *Building Research & Information*, 1-20. https://doi.org/10.1080/09613218.2020.1784702

Waheed, M., Klobas, J. E., & Ain, N. (2020). Unveiling knowledge quality, researcher satisfaction, learning, and loyalty. *Information Technology & People.* https://doi.org/10.1108/ITP-07-2018-0345

Weller, M (2011). *The Digital Scholar: How technology is transforming scholarly practice.* London: Bloomsbury. https://doi.org/10.5040/9781849666275

Zawacki-Richter, O., & Naidu, S. (2016). Mapping research trends from 35 years of publications in Distance Education. *Distance Education, 37*(3), 245-269.

Zawacki-Richter, O., & Qayyum, A. (2019*). Open and distance education in Asia, Africa and the Middle East: National perspectives in a digital age.* Springer Nature.

DEVELOPMENT OF ONLINE EDUCAMPS DURING THE COVID-19 PANDEMIC

Sólveig Jakobsdóttir, Hróbjartur Árnason, University of Iceland., Iceland

Abstract

Educamps are informal events where people gather to teach each other and discuss, for example, how to apply new technologies, software, equipment and tools, in hands-on learning contexts with opportunities for networking (Leal Fonseca, 2011). From 2012, educamps have become increasingly popular in Iceland as a useful method for teachers' professional development as well as in teacher education. As a response to restraints on gatherings due to the COVID19 pandemic, and a nationwide rush to online teaching in the spring of 2020, academic staff at University of Iceland – School of Education (UI) and at the University of Akureyri (UA) decided to experiment with moving this type of event from physical locations to online spaces, and thus to support teachers who suddenly needed to move their teaching online. In this poster session we will describe the reactions and views expressed by participants of three online educamps attended by over 400 people across Iceland and their assessment of this type of professional development (online survey participation after each event was 22-35%). The majority thought the online educamps participation had been (very) useful (79%, 74%, 90%) or considerably useful (17%, 24%, 10%). Almost all survey participants liked this type of professional development very much (68%, 67%, 86%) or liked it (27%, 33%, 14%). The majority expressed willingness to take advantage of this type of professional development in the future and several were interested in organising online educamps of a similar type themselves. Answers to an open-ended question revealed, for example, that participants from rural areas were especially happy with online educamps which were open to anyone regardless of location. Early results indicate that this type of professional development can be useful for teachers.

Keywords: Online educamps, teachmeets, teacher professional development, COVID-19

Introduction

With increasing pressure to keep current regarding technological developments in changing pedagogical landscapes, new forms of teacher training and professional development are needed (Henderikx & Jansen, 2018). In 2012, Icelandic teacher educators, in collaboration with practicing teachers and ICT school leaders, started organising educamps focusing on ICT in education for teacher students and practicing teachers (Jakobsdóttir, 2020). These types of events could be classified as "un-conferences" (Hale & Bessette, 2016) or "a less-structured opportunity for participants to learn and grow by sharing individual expertise in a variety of ways that reflect participant interests, preferences, skill sets, and needs." The term *edcamp* has also been used (Carpenter, 2016; Carpenter & Linton, 2018; Carpenter & MacFarlane, 2018) when the main target group involves educators (Carpenter & MacFarlane, 2018; p.71). Other labels include playdate (Schlesinger, 2017) and teachmeet (Turner, 2017).

In Iceland these hands-on workshops have typically taken place at schools or universities where participants take turns being in the role of teachers or students with an emphasis on peer learning and networking and the development of competencies in the use of educational technologies, however with a varied degree of structure and format. Educamps have received positive reactions from participants who tend to enjoy the experiences and claim considerable learning gains (Jakobsdóttir, 2018; 2019; 2020). They have become increasingly popular and the practice has spread across Iceland for the last years. This type of professional development has also been successful as a method for professional development related to the use of ICT in teaching and learning in other countries (Carpenter, 2016; Carpenter & Linton, 2018; Carpenter & MacFarlane, 2018; Leal Fonseca, 2011).

During the COVID-19 crisis in the spring, schools in Iceland as elsewhere were faced with school buildings closing and teaching activities moving entirely online (at the upper secondary or university level) or coping with restrictions on regular school activities with increased online teaching and learning. Seven teacher educators at University of

Iceland and University of Akureyri decided to explore ways to support teachers and as part of that effort organised three educamp-style events online with a special focus on distance and online teaching and learning, tips, tricks and methods which would be useful to teachers who were forced to radically change modalities of their daily teaching routines. The main goal was thus to support educators confronted with school buildings closing or restrictions of regular educational activities and therefore needing to change their practices. In this paper/poster we will describe the organisation of the online educamps and then report participants' reactions.

The online educamps

The idea to develop online educamps in the spring 2020 started with two teacher educators working at University of Iceland (UI) and University of Akureyri (UA) (Jakobsdóttir, 2020) confronted with having to move online educamps, they had planned to have on-site in March 2020 with their students. They both introduced their ideas and plans in mid-March in a Facebook group focusing on school development (with ca. 5000 Icelandic educators) where a lot of discussion was taking place at the time about how teachers could change their practice during the COVID-19 crisis. School closures and other restrictions had started a few day earlier. The idea to hold online educamps got very positive reactions from participants in online forums, so a collaboration started involving the two teacher educators and five of their colleagues (Sólveig Jakobsdóttir, Sólveig Zophoníasdóttir, Hróbjartur Árnason, Ingvar Sigurgeirsson, Kristín Dýrfjörð, Salvör Gissurardóttir, Svava Pétursdóttir). There were consultations and assistance provided by Reykjavík Municipality Department of Education and Youth, The Directorate of Education, The Icelandic Teachers' Union, The Education and Training Service Centre, and the EducationPlaza.

Three online educamps were organised in the spring semester 2020. They were open and free to anyone to participate. The first one, on March 26, was hosted less than two weeks from the original Facebook interactions. The programme was organized with 4 25 min. sessions in the afternoon with 6 Zoom parallel meeting rooms open during each session, providing room for 24 slots. The timeframe for the program was set up in a table in GoogleDocs a few days before the event and advertised on social media. Anyone could enter a session proposal directly into the program indicating what they wanted to discuss or introduce (e.g. digital tools, online teaching methods, elearning materials). During the first event there were altogether 24 contributions from 22 people. Approximately 250 people visited one or more of the teachers/guides during the event including a joint "fish-bowl"-type discussion which was organised at the end. These attendance estimates are based on attendance records in Zoom – however many did not give a full name and/or could have used a psydonym. During the second two events, one of the hosts visited all rooms three times, in the beginning, middle and end.

The second online educamp was organised three weeks later, on April 16, in a similar style as the first one and the third one May 7 (around this time meeting restrictions were eased up). The April event had only three sessions with 5 parallel meeting rooms, so 15 were slots available and the last educamp had two sessions with six parallel meeting rooms (12 slots). The slots also filled up during both the following events, with 17 people doing introductions and about 210 attending the April event and 14 doing introductions in the May educamp and about 60 attending. Altogether we estimate that well over 400 people attended one or more of the three events with the 51 introductions by 39 persons. Sometimes there were two people introducing together and sometimes one person did more than one introduction either at the same event or at different events. The majority of the sessions were recorded and made openly available at a website (GoogleSites) the team developed.

Participants and their reactions

After each of the online educamps participants were invited to submit their reactions in an online anonymous survey. There were 57 participants in the first survey, 70 in the second, and 21 in the third (estimated about 22-35% participation rate).

Participants' background: school level/learner groups and previous educamp experience

Participants were asked to indicate how their work related to school levels and or learner groups. It was possible to check more than one answer. Most of the participants worked on the primary or lower secondary level. Over 80% of the participants in event 2 and 3 were connected with that level and about half of the participants of event 1. People connected with preschool were 3 to 13% with the highest percentage in event 2. People connected with the upper secondary school level were 1 to 19% with the lowest percentage in event 2. People from the university level were 9 to 14% and connection to adult/vocational education was 4 to 25%, the highest ratio was in event 1.

Participant's previous experience of educamps varied but the majority reported previous experience of educamps. A quarter to one third even had experience of 10 or more educamps event whereas 5 to 28% had no experience.

In addition, survey participants were asked after event 2 whether they had also attended the first event and 53.6% reported they had. Moreover, survey participants were asked after event 2 whether they had also attended the first event and 53.6% reported that they had. The survey participants were asked after event 3 whether they had also attended the earlier two. About 63% reported attending the first event and 80% the second event.

Participants' experiences: usefulness, enjoyment, attendance and interest for future events

A great majority of survey participants reported the events as useful. About 79% of the participants in event 1 said they had very much (42%) or much (37%) use of their participation. About 74% of the participants in event 2 thought the same (27% very much, 47% much). Similarly, 90% of participants in event 3 indicated they had very much (33%) or much (57%)

use of their participation. Furthermore, 10 to 24% reported considerable use and hardly anyone little or very little use (1 or 2 participants in the earlier two events).

The vast majority of participants appreciated this form of professional development. Over two thirds of the participants in event 1 and 2 (68% and 67% respectively) rated the format very h and 86% of the third event. In addition, 27%, 33%, and 14% of participants in events 1 to 3 reported they liked it well. No survey participant rated the experience as bad or very bad. But a few (5%) from event 5 were neutral.

It varied widely how many sessions the participants attended. Event 1 had the most sessions, four with six presentations each and a plenum "fish-bowl"-style session at the end of the day. About 16% of the survey participants had only attended one session, 17% two, 10% three, 36% four, and 21% all five sessions. Event 2 had three sessions with five introductions each and a "coffee-room" open for "happy hour" at the end as well as being open during the three earlier session. About 6% of survey participants had attended one session, 31% two sessions, 47% three sessions, and 16% all three as well as visiting the "coffee room". Event three had two sessions with six introductions each and a "happy hour" in the "coffee room" at the end. About 14% attended one session, 33% two, and 52% all three sessions.

Survey participants were also asked how likely they would be to attend potential future events of this sort. Everyone thought it was certain, very likely or likely. About 53% of participants of event 1 were 100% certain, 38% after event 2 and 57% after event 3. In addition, 39% of participants of event 1 thought it very likely, 48% after event 2, and 43% after event 3. Finally, 9% after event 1 and 15% after event 2 thought it likely.

Finally survey participants after events 2 and 3 were asked how interested they were in organising educamps online at their institutions for co-workers, students or others. The majority had a considerable or high interest but 47% of event 2 participants had little or very little interest and 33% of the participants of event 3.

Conclusions and continuing work

As can be seen from the results above, the Icelandic school community reacted very positively to our experiment during the first COVID-19 wave. The team of teacher educators involved in this project have since then received funding from University of Iceland to continue this work, develop this model further with a design-based research approach and to publish a handbook for practitioners who themselves want to offer this type of professional development.

References

Carpenter, J. P. (2016). Unconference professional development: Edcamp participant perceptions and motivations for attendance. *Professional Development in Education, 42*(1), 78-99. https://doi.org/10.1080/19415257.2015.1036303

Carpenter, J. P., & Linton, J. N. (2018). Educators' perspectives on the impact of Edcamp unconference professional learning. *Teaching and Teacher Education, 73*, 56-69. https://doi.org/10.1016/j.tate.2018.03.014

Carpenter, J. P., & MacFarlane, M. R. (2018). Educator perceptions of district-mandated Edcamp unconferences. *Teaching and Teacher Education, 75*, 71-82. https://doi.org/10.1016/j.tate.2018.06.002

Hale, E., & Bessette, L. S. (2016). New frontiers: Exploring the power and possibilities of the unconference as a transformative approach to faculty development. *The Journal of Faculty Development, 30*(2), 9-15.

Henderikx, P., & Jansen, D. (2018). *The Changing Pedagogical Landscape: In search of patterns in policies and practices of new modes of teaching and learning.* Retrieved from https://tinyurl.com/CPLreport2018

Jakobsdóttir, S. (2018). Educamps in distance education: professional development and peer learning for student teachers in ICT. In A. Volungeviciene & A. Szucs (Eds.), *Exploring the Micro, Meso and Macro: Navigating between dimensions in the digital learning landscape – Conference Proceedings of the EDEN 2018 Annual Conference* (pp. 501-507). Genoa: European Distance and E-Learning Network.

Jakobsdóttir, S. (2019). ICT in teacher education: Educamps and peer learning. In E. M. Varonis (Ed.), *International conference on information communication technologies in education – proceedings* (pp. 1-9). Chania, Crete: ICICTE.

Jakobsdóttir, S. (2020). Menntabúðir í starfsþróun kennara: Geta þær virkað á netinu? [Educamps in teachers' professional development: Can they work online?]. *Skólaþræðir, 9*(4).

Leal Fonseca, D. (2011). EduCamp Colombia: Social networked learning for teacher training. *The International Review of Research in Open and Distance Learning, 12*(3), 60-79.

Schlesinger, E. (2017). PD Your Way: 10 teacher-sourced ways to do professional development – anywhere, anytime. *Scholastic Teacher, 127*(2), 40-43.

Turner, K. (2017). *How to organise a successful TeachMeet.* Retrieved from https://eic.rsc.org/ideas/how-to-organise-asuccessful-teachmeet/3007851.article

AUGMENTED REALITY IN EDUCATION: DESIGNING RESOURCES AND TEACHING INNOVATION

Ricardo Monteiro, António Quintas-Mendes, Laboratory of Distance Education and eLearning (LE@D), Universidade Aberta, Portugal

Abstract

Teachers and students in the education system are confronted with a few challenges that essentially refer to the way in which the increasingly imperceptible fusion between the analogue and digital world, between the physical and the virtual, and between presence and distance, is managed. This framework is the result of the evolution and increasingly easier access to immersive technologies such as virtual reality, augmented reality and mixed reality. A scenario that imposes research on the training and adaptation of educational agents, more specifically teachers and students, regarding how they can implement these new innovative solutions in order to develop skills that allow them to participate and interact in a global world. This study presents a set of actions that have been developed over the last two years, where teachers from different areas have been encouraged to reflect, use and develop augmented reality resources. The gap that still exists between technological evolution and the evolution of digital competences and the practices that are used in classroom activities is remarkable. Although it is noted that they are resources little present in schools, there is unanimous recognition that this technology has characteristics that allow the creation of new dynamics of knowledge construction and digital training of the educational community.

Keywords: Augmented Reality; Digital Skills; Immersive Technologies; Education.

Introduction

This article is part of the PhD thesis on Distance Education and eLearning, Open University and its research is part of the Research Unit 4372/FCT Laboratory of Distance Education and eLearning, Open University, Portugal.

The emerging digital systems have given way to the exploration of new dimensions and the possibility of innovative frameworks that challenge the transformation and creation of learning experiences, giving them greater interactivity and new dimensions. A scenario that imposes on teachers, hoping that they will be able to present innovative solutions and develop, in the school community, the capacity to participate and interact in a global world (Coutinho & Lisbôa, 2011).

Gomes, Figueiredo, Bidarra, and Gomes (2016) identify three trends in Education: (a) "the passage from the physical space of the classroom to many other spaces, whether presential, virtual or of mixed typology (...)"; (b) "learning mediated by information and communication technologies (...)"; (c) "and the implementation of gamification strategies in the educational process".

And in this context, it is important to highlight the recognition that the same researchers give when they associate to these strategies "technologies that fascinate students, such as Augmented Reality (AR) [...], they gain a very promising way of intrinsically motivation in students" (Gomes, Figueiredo, Bidarra, & Gomes, 2016).

There are several authors and studies that advocate Augmented Reality (AR) "as a key component in future technological learning didactic objects" (Gomes et al., 2016; p.459). Despite their different natures and methodological approaches, the conclusions of these studies are unanimous in recognizing the potential and unique characteristics of this technology. The fact that, at the same time, it enables immersive and contextualized experiments with real elements is pointed out as one of the main differentiating features in relation to other technologies, namely in relation to Virtual Reality (VR).

This identifies the possibility of being confronted with a technology that can increase motivation, both in teachers, in the development of educational activities, and in students, in the realization of these activities and the construction of knowledge.

These emerging environments foresee new opportunities for Education. Teachers, students and other professionals involved in education are challenged to find "strategies to integrate this learning model that can motivate teachers to transform their teaching and learning habits" (Donato, 2014; p.22).

However, Bower, Howe, McCredie, Robinson, and Grover (2013) warn that there is a gap between advances in AR technology research and research in Education, thus identifying the difficulty that the educational community sometimes has in keeping up with this evolution. These context alert to the importance of future AR research happens not only perspective as a new technology, but also to the concern to involve it in teaching processes and the development of learning experiences.

This is the problem that leads us to consider the possibility that this technology, when used in an environment that integrates ubiquitous learning experiences (u-learning), may acquire greater relevance and lead to the effective enrichment of learning and generate new pedagogical approaches.

It is with this assumption that this study focuses on the theme of Augmented Reality, and its main objective is to understand the potentialities and challenges that this technology confers in the redesign of pedagogical practices, in the creation of learning experiences and in the training of teachers and students of digital skills.

Augmented Reality in Education

The innovative features and new functionalities present in technologies must be taken on by teachers and educational policy makers as properties to encourage the acceptance of their exploitation and insertion into the educational system.

With the increasing sophistication of mobile devices and their massification, m-learning (Barbante & Oliveira, 2015) becomes more important in classrooms, adding the characteristic of mobility as its main difference and value. It is a fact that, in the last decade, the evolution of mobile technologies has revolutionised and driven the emergence of new educational "paradigms (Barbante & Oliveira, 2015). The same authors point out that "this mobile and tactile technology brings enormous challenges", stressing that "we can learn anywhere, at any time and in many ways, in a modality called ubiquitous learning" (Santaella, 2013; as cited in Barbante & Oliveira, 2015; p. 164).

AR applications and resources have benefited from this increase in m-learning in teaching processes, recognising their potential as a tool for opening up to new learning processes and environments (Oliveira, 2016). Although there are several equipment that allow the visualisation of Augmented Reality, such as AR/VR glasses, touch screens, holographic reproductions, it is through smartphones and tables that it can be most easily used and experienced.

According to Gomes, Figueiredo, Bidarra, and Gomes (2016) this technology will constitute "a key component in future learning objects". The unique potential of this technology is recognised by the fact that it "combines and unites various complementary digital information media (three-dimensional models, images, audio, video, text files, etc.) with real-world objects" (Gomes et al., 2016), thus creating immersive and contextualised experiences. Its use in enriching teaching processes and the growing interest it has generated in teachers and researchers not only creates opportunities, but also presents numerous challenges to society as a whole (Gomes, 2015). Figueiredo, Amado, Bidarra, and Carriera (2015) highlights the possibility for most young people and teachers to "develop activities that take advantage of the potential of AR technologies to improve learning experiences".

Although this technology has been under development for several years, it still takes on an experimental character, which reminds us of the importance of enumerating the benefits and limitations that are detected as a pedagogical tool used to enrich learning.

Table 1 identifies some of the benefits and limitations of the AR.

We are witnessing a time when many young people and teachers can develop activities that take advantage of the potential of AR technologies to improve their teaching and learning experiences. However, their use not only creates opportunities but also presents numerous challenges to the whole society (Gomes, 2015).

According to Costa (2014), there are two possible approaches for the development of AR applications: "the first is by making direct use of programming and the second by making use of an AR authoring tool" (Costa, 2014, p. 5).

Table 1: Benefits and limitations of the AR

Benefits of the AR	Limitations of the AR
the teacher has the opportunity to reduce the gap between what is taught and what is learned by the student (Costa & Cruz, 2015; p.121);	the accuracy of the GPS system of mobile devices limits the display of the location of learning objects – teachers should consider the size of learning objects and the distance between them (Chiang, Yang, & Hwang, 2014; p.362);
the interaction between students, allows for the sharing of ideas, making the pedagogical content dealt with in class better understood, at the same time as collaborative, innovative and creative skills are developed (Costa & Cruz, 2015; p.121);	the provision of instantaneous information or personalised guidance, teachers need to spend considerable time developing learning processes and digital materials to provide learning support (Chiang, Yang, & Hwang, 2014; p.362);
learning is optimized, and brain areas activated, essential factors to minimize the inefficiency of traditional educational systems (Costa & Cruz, 2015; p.121);	difficulties in maintenance and the need for more attention to virtual information and the fact that AR is an intrusive technology (Bacca et al., 2014; p.146);

increasing students' interest and motivation to use these technologies for different applications by improving collaboration between actors in the teaching/learning process (Oliveira, 2016; p.444); enables contextualised learning experiences closer to reality (Jorge et al., 2012; p.305); allows the manipulation of virtual objects in the real world in an immersive way, even filling in the practicality often dissociated from e-Learning (Jorge et al., 2012; p.305); better performance, motivation, student involvement and positive attitudes towards learning (Bacca, Baldiris, Fabregat, Graf, & Kinshuk, 2014; p.146); enabling learning in contexts that are impossible or difficult to experience in real life (Ferreira, 2015; p.112).	the technology still has some limitations and is constantly being updated (Ferreira, 2015, p. 112);

The application of AR in education presents a very large development potential (Zorzal, Jorge, & Costa, 2018), and when combined with the massification and acceptance that digital technologies and mobile devices have acquired by those in charge of the education system, it combines with an excellent opportunity to explore AR in education.

Research Method

The main objective of this study is to respond to some challenges that are pointed to the use of AR in the enrichment of teaching processes and learning experiences.

This scenario establishes the need to create research opportunities that allow:

- the understanding of the ubiquitous dimension of AR and its contribution in enriching learning experiences in different educational spaces;
- an approach that raises the AR beyond its simple analysis of interactions and privileges its qualities as a pedagogical tool to access and visualize educational digital resources;
- the creation of spaces for reflection and training actions in the AR;
- the design and development of AR resources;
- the analysis of the use of AR in different educational contexts and the perception that its agents have of this technology.

This study presents a proposal aimed at the (re)design of learning experiences and the exploration of new educational paradigms, in order to answer the following questions: "How does Augmented Reality promote the development of ubiquitous learning experiences in Education?" and "How does the use of Augmented Reality contribute to the acquisition of digital skills by teachers and students?

The empirical study is divided into two phases, and due to the characteristics of each one, different methodologies are needed. The first phase, given the nature of product development that is foreseen, refers to a Human-Centred Design (HCD) approach, valuing the proximity between those who conceive the activity, produce the application and use it. The second phase adopts a "multiple-explanatory descriptive case study" methodology considered by several authors (Lee, Yarger, Lincoln, Guba, Gravemeijer, and Shulman) as the best option for a naturalistic research in education.

The selection of participants was made intentionally on the basis of "pragmatic and theoretical criteria (...), seeking not uniformity, but maximum variations" (Bravo, 1998; as cited in Coutinho & Chaves, 2002). Participants in this study are teachers of primary and secondary education, students and those responsible for the educational service of the Internacional Museum of Contemporary Sculpture (MIEC), Santo Tirso, giving it the plurality with regard to educational agents.

Over two years they have been realised:

- AR resource planning and development workshops;
- meetings (encont[RA]r) of reflection with the participation of more than 200 teachers and several speakers from different countries who brought their perspectives as experts in the field of the development of AR technology and Educational Technology;
- interviews, in order to collect testimonies of AR resource use and development;
- records of AR resources that have been developed by teachers and students as part of their teaching activities.

Conclusions

If "the demands and expectations of users, who are increasingly prone to innovation, are opening the doors to increased reality" (Magalhães, 2010), new opportunities must be created in the transformation of current education and learning systems. The use of this technology in educational contexts has, in recent years, become increasingly evident in the research in Education, but a very residual use of such resources is still identified.

For both teachers and students, the difficulties presented to develop and/or make profitable the AR resources they currently have at their disposal are evident. There is a common lack of knowledge about this technology, and initiatives to promote and clarify the potential of Augmented Reality in Education are considered fundamental.

However, most teachers recognise AR technology as a pedagogical tool promoting ubiquitous teaching and amplifying learning spaces.

In recent years, the development and evolution that the AR technology has been achieving in several areas is notorious, and Education, despite taking a longer progression, is beginning to present strategies that add these technologies to its pedagogical practices.

It is very important to continue reflecting on the use of these immersive technologies and to deepen their valences and opportunities in teaching and learning processes.

References

Bacca, J., Baldiris, S., Fabregat, R., Graf, S., & Kinshuk. (2014). Augmented Reality Trends in Education: A Systematic Review of Research and Applications. *Educational Technology & Society, 17*(4), 133-149.

Barbante, C., & Oliveira, L. (2015). As Tecnologias Móveis no Processo de Ensino e Aprendizagem. In M. J. Gomes, A. J. Osório, & L. Valente (Eds,), *Challenges 2015: Meio Século de TIC na Educação* (pp. 163-173). Braga: Universidade do Minho. Centro de Competência TIC do Instituto de Educação.

Bower, M., Howe, C., McCredie, N., Robinson, A., & Grover, D. (2013). Augmented reality in Education - Cases, places, and potentials. *Proceedings of the 2013 IEEE 63rd Annual Conference International Council for Education Media (ICEM).* Retrieved from http://dx.doi.org/10.1109/cicem.2013.6820176

Chiang, T.-H.-C., Yang, S.-J.-H., & Hwang, G.-J. (2014). An Augmented Reality-based Mobile Learning System to Improve Students' Learning Achievements and Motivations in Natural Science Inquiry Activities. *Educational Technology & Society, 17*(4), 352-365.

Costa, M. A. (2014). *Potencialidades da realidade aumentada no ensino e aprendizagem: um estudo com alunos do 7º ano de escolaridade* (Mestrado em Ensino de Informática). Universidade Católica Portuguesa. Retrieved from http://hdl.handle.net/10400.14/18164

Costa, M. & Cruz, S. (2015). A Utilização da Realidade Aumentada para Aprender História: um estudo com alunos do 3.º CEB. Proceedings of the *Challenges 2015: Meio Século de TIC na Educação,* 119-135. Braga: Universidade do Minho. Centro de Competência TIC do Instituto de Educação.

Coutinho, C., & Chaves, H. (2002). O estudo de caso na investigação em Tecnologia Educativa em Portugal. *Revista Portuguesa De Educação, 15*(1), 221-243. Retrieved from https://repositorium.sdum.uminho.pt/retrieve/940/ClaraCoutinho.pdf

Coutinho, C., & Lisbôa, E. (2011). Sociedade da Informação, do Conhecimento e da Aprendizagem: Desafios para a Educação no Século XXI. *Revista De Educação, XVIII*(1), 5-22. Retrieved from https://repositorium.sdum.uminho.pt/bitstream/1822/14854/1/Revista_Educação,VolXVIII,nº1_5-22.pdf

Donato, D. (2014). *Aprendizagem com Mobilidade: Os tablets em Sala de Aula Suscitando Novas Práticas Pedagógicas* (Mestrado em Educação). Universidade de Lisboa.

Ferreira, J. (2015). *Design para realidade aumentada: um estudo em contexto educativo* (Doutoramento em BelasArtes). Universidade de Lisboa.

Figueiredo, M., Amado, N., Bidarra, J., & Carreira, S. (2015). A realidade aumentada na aprendizagem da matemática no ensino secundário. *Proceedings of the Conferência Internacional do Espaço Matemático em Língua Portuguesa,* 1-5. Coimbra: CIEMeLP. Retrieved from http://repositorioaberto.uab.pt/bitstream/10400.2/4566/1/CiEMeLP-2015_paper_145.pdf

Gomes, C., Figueiredo, M., Bidarra, J., & Gomes, J. (2016). *Realidade aumentada e gamificação: desenvolvimento de aumentações num manual escolar de educação musical.* Paper presented at the 3º Encontro sobre Jogos e Mobile Learning – EJML 2016. Coimbra: Universidade de Coimbra. Retrieved from http://hdl.handle.net/10400.2/5306

Gomes, J. D. C. (2015). *Realidade aumentada em manuais escolares de educação visual no 2º Ciclo do Ensino Básico* (Mestrado em Promoção da Leitura e Bibliotecas Escolares). Universidade de Aveiro.

Jorge, N., Gaspar, P., & Morgado, L. (2012). Realidade aumentada mediada por tecnologias móveis no ensino da enfermagem. *Proceedings of the Encontro sobre Jogos e Mobile Learning,* 304-310. Braga: Centro de Investigação em Educação (CIEd). Retrieved from http://www.fpce.uc.pt/ejml2014/Atas EJML-2012.pdf

Magalhães, P. (2010). *Realidade Aumentada Aplicada ao Processo de Ensino/Aprendizagem.* (Mestrado em Engenharia Informática). Instituto Superior de Engenharia do Porto.

Oliveira, D. (2016). A utilização da Realidade Aumentada como estratégia de suporte ao ensino da informática. *Proceedings of the 3.º Encontro sobre Jogos e Mobile Learning,* 441-447. Coimbra: Universidade de Coimbra. Faculdade de Psicologia e de Ciências da Educação, LabTE. Retrieved from http://hdl.handle.net/10316/31171

Zorzal, E., Jorge, J., & Costa, G. (2018). Desafios e Aplicações da Realidade Aumentada Móvel na Educação. *Revista Novas Tecnologias na Educação, 16*(2), 1-10. doi:10.22456/1679-1916.89239

TEACHERS AND LEARNERS CHANGING ROLES IN A GLOBAL TECHNOLOGY-MEDIATED ENVIRONMENT

Fátima Carneiro, Luísa Aires, Laboratory of Distance Education and eLearning (LE@D), Universidade Aberta, Portugal

Abstract

This poster addresses the theme of Teachers and learners changing roles in a global technology-mediated environment.

Given the context of the COVID-19 Pandemic, it is imperative to develop and implement strategies that mitigate its educational impact. Differences between school systems in a global context and their ability to design and implement appropriate educational responses can generate more learning opportunities around the world.

This poster presents some data and reflections resulting from an ongoing research on Global Education in a European School in an international context. For this purpose, a mixed research methodology was used, with the application of a closed answer questionnaire to students and a semi-structured interview with teachers.

Partial data on the perspectives of students and teachers regarding Global Education and some of the skills that this educational approach presupposes are analysed.

The results, still provisional, of the research reveal that they are the international matrix of the school under study, promoting global education, with a strong anchor in intercultural competences. However, there are limitations in the use of digital technologies and the Internet in the school context that can compromise the full dynamisation of this educational perspective.

Keywords: Global Education; Global competences; Digital skills.

Introduction

In the face of the COVID-19 Pandemic, the importance of formulating educational responses that are consistent with a crisis that introduces significant changes in learning opportunities worldwide is highlighted.

Taking into account the educational needs in a global context, it is up to the school to look for solutions and give appropriate responses to the characteristics of each school community, also at the technological and digital skills level. In this context, global education becomes one of the essential pillars in terms of educational decision-making and in the search for effective educational responses, through participatory strategies and methods, which refer to a change at the local level with a global influence.

Global competences, a concept linked to that of global education, point us to the ability to understand global interdependence. Its acquisition is fundamental for participation in a global society, focusing on promoting learning in an interdependent world, with an approach focused on building a more just and sustainable world (Reimers, 2013; Bourn, 2014). From the range of global skills, we highlight the importance of digital skills, as the absence of these skills triggers the impossibility of participating in a global, networked society (Castells, 2006).

Global Education and Digital Skills

Global education stands out for its scope and interdisciplinary nature and brings together the agendas of different fields of education, providing context for broad curricular structures, with educational activities oriented to global scenarios. This perspective of education points to a common future, in a fairer and more sustainable world, with better living conditions for all, locally and globally.

Global education can play an important role in the creation of new methods where social movements and learning processes based on dialogue and cooperation, can modify the established rules of the global economy, restoring human dignity as a central value. This perspective of Education underlies a set of purposes that can help to align the curriculum with the real world, making it easier for teachers and students to better understand the relationship between what is learned at school and outside school (Silva, 2010; 2019; Reimers, 2020).

Indeed, global competences refer to a learning of multiple, diverse spectrum, valuing the plural and the particular, with the purpose of promoting open and effective interactions with people of different origins, based on a shared respect for human dignity.

The idea of communication and information has been imposing itself according to its specificity and autonomy, and also as a central idea of social life, highlighting the role of global communications, from the press to the Internet (Cardoso, 2014; p.4). Therefore, new concepts and new approaches have emerged, highlighting a trend of more participative social digital media, with an enhanced importance for new forms of communication, expression, living, learning and working. With a view to preparing people for a global multicultural and digital world, education promotes knowledge, skills and practices, of learning inside and outside schools. Thus, digital technologies are fundamental for the restructuring of most contemporary formal education environments, with the mission of supporting and encouraging active citizenship and self-expression in democratic societies (Gutiérrez & Tyner, 2012). Effectively, digital competence, generally understood as the ability to use digital technologies in the context of work, leisure and communication (From, 2017) is recognized as one of the essential competences for lifelong learning, being referenced by UNESCO and the European Union, in documents of a strategic and political nature, associated with educational agents, namely students and teachers (Santos, Azevedo, & Pedro, 2015; p.27; Aires, Palmeiro, & Pereda, 2019; p.14).

Empirical study

The empirical study we present results from a broader investigation that has objectives:

- identify global education practices with students and teachers in a European school;
- know the approaches used to stimulate learning among students from different cultures;
- collect information on the influence of global competences in the development of global education.

In this study, it is intended to obtain possible answers to the question: What are the perspectives of students and teachers at a European School on Global Education?

Research context and sample

The research takes place in a European School. It involves 154 students from Primary and Secondary Education and 4 teachers, 2 teachers from the primary cycle and 2 from the secondary cycle.

Methodology: Information collection techniques

We opted for a mixed research methodology. For this purpose, a closed answer questionnaire was built and applied to students. The questionnaire consists of twenty questions, with Likert-type answer items, on a scale of 1 to 4, and some questions with a dichotomous scale "Yes" or "No".

Semi-structured interviews were also conducted with teachers. For conducting the interviews, a guide was built based on two major blocks: Global education and global skills.

In this presentation we emphasize the categories: Global Education Initiatives and practices in School, Commitment to the planet, Participation in multicultural projects and Projects on the web.

Data analysis and discussion

The data resulting from the questionnaires applied to students were analysed using descriptive and inferential statistical methods, using SPSS (Statistics Version 26). In turn, for the analysis of teachers' speeches, they resorted to qualitative content analysis (Bardin, 1977), with the support of Nvivo (version 11).

Multicultural Education Practices

Multicultural Education at school starts from teachers' respect for cultural difference and diversity. Indeed, 79.8% of students consider that the majority of teachers value students equally, regardless of their cultural or linguistic origins:

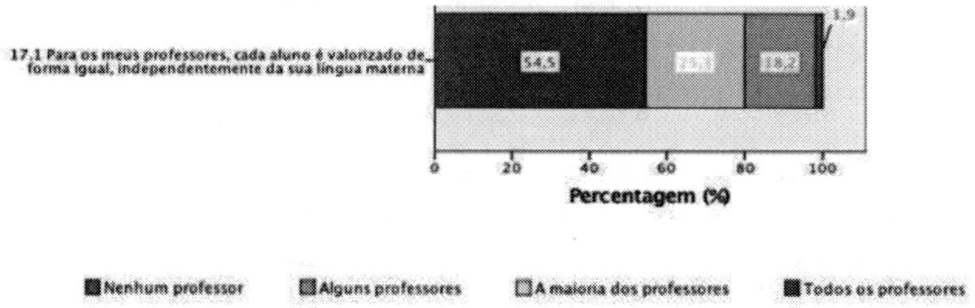

Figure 1. Multicultural education practices at school

School and Commitment to the Planet

Commitment to people and the planet is also a dimension present in students' practices, especially in those attending secondary education. Almost all students (n = 143) belong to an environmental group or organization and more than half (67.5%) keep themselves informed about different events through social networks, namely Twitter, Facebook or Instagram.

Table 1: Chi-Square test results to verify if there is a relationship between the variables related to commitments and obligations to people and the planet and the level of education of the participants

Relationships between variables	Chi-square	df	Value of p
Education level * I keep informed about different events through social networks	25.062	1	<0.001**

Participation Multicultural Projects and Openness to Multicultural Experiences

Teachers, when asked about this issue, value above all the practices of global education at school and, in particular, participation in multicultural projects in network with other schools:

> *"We also have the BRUMUM project. I think this organization was an excellent idea. This project is through the European School of Brussels II, and at the moment, there are already fifteen countries participating. This is surely the major global education project. This project allows an exchange between several schools in Europe, in this case there are fifteen schools in contact." (E3)*

> *"Now, what is the 'China Exchange'? It is an exchange that started to be promoted a few years ago, with the Director at the time, he was Irish. (...) It is to realize that the school is inserted in a community, in a neighbourhood, and that it is necessary to make partnerships with everything that we have around us. And what we have here, is the Chinese Embassy. (...) until there was a time when he thought it would be interesting, both for our students and for young Chinese people." (E2)*

Projects on the web

The use of the Internet does not seem to be a priority for the four teachers. In fact, only two of these teachers highlight them, pointing out the tools they use and the virtualities they have:

> *"Yes. We have 'Teams', which is a kind of educational community, which is done at the class level. But we can create other groups. But this year I only have students of Portuguese 4, and since their Portuguese level is still very insipient, I haven't launched them yet. But I have my Latin students who already use it. It started now, is connected to the Office 365 Platform, and is very easy to access." (E2)*

Final considerations

The European school under study allows us to conclude, still provisionally, that the international dimension of its educational project, the experiences of the teachers who teach there and the different socio-cultural contexts of the students who attend it are relevant elements for the promotion of Global Education and the competencies associated with it. Respect for diversity, commitment to people and the planet and participation in multicultural network projects are important areas in the global education practices promoted at this school.

Considering that digital skills and, in particular, Internet use skills, are part of the wide range of global skills, it appears, however, that this assumption does not seem to be a priority in the curricula and practices of these teachers . While students, especially older ones, turn to social networks to find out about global issues, the use of the Internet and the development of skills for its good use, this does not emerge as a priority in teachers' discourse.

References

Aires, L., Palmeiro, R., & Pereda, V. (2019). Das Competências de uso das Tecnologias Digitais ao exercício pleno da Cidadania Digital: os casos do Alentejo e do País Basco. *E@D – Revista de Educação a Distância e Elearning, 2*(1), 9-25.

Bardin, L. (1977). *Análise de Conteúdo.* Lisboa: Edições 70.

Bourn, D. (2014). *The Theory and Practice of Global Learning.* Research Paper No.11. London: Development Education Research Centre, Institute of Education in partnership with the Global Learning Programme.

Cardoso, G. (2014). *Da Comunicação em Massa à Comunicação em Rede: Modelos Comunicacionais e a Sociedade de Informação.* Portal da Comunicação InCom-UAB· Lições do portal. ISSN 2014-0576

Castells, M. (Ed.) (2006). *La sociedad red: una visión global.*

From, J. (2017). Pedagogical digital competence—between values, knowledge and skills. *Higher Education Studies, 7*(2), 43. doi:10.5539/hes.v7n2p43

Gutiérrez, A. & Tyner, K., (2012). Media Education, Media Literacy and Digital Competence. *Comunicar: Scientific Journal of Media Education.*

Reimers, F. M. (2013). *Assessing Global Education: an Opportunity for the OECD.*

Reimers, F. M. (2020). *Audacious Education Purposes-How Governments Transform the Goals of Education Systems.*

Santos, R., Azevedo, J., & Pedro, L. (2015). *Literacia(s) Digital(ais): Definições, perspetivas e desafios.* Aveiro: Universidade de Aveiro.

Silva, M. C. (Ed.) (2010). *Guia Prático para a Educação Global: Um manual para compreender e implementar a Educação Global.* Lisboa: Centro Norte-Sul do Conselho da Europa.

Silva, M. C. (Ed.) (2019). *Global Education Guidelines, Concepts, and methodologies on global education for educators and policy makers.* Lisbon: North-South Centre of the Council of Europe.

Acknowledgement

This project is part of a doctoral thesis integrated in the R &D unit 4372/FCT – LE@D.

DISTANCE LEARNING VERSUS EMERGENCY REMOTE LEARNING: PORTUGUESE SCHOOLS IN A TURNING POINT FOR DIGITAL TRANSFORMATION?

Ana Paula Afonso, Antonieta Rocha, Maria João Spilker, Lina Morgado, LE@D – Laboratory of Distance Education & eLearning, Universidade Aberta, Portugal

Abstract

The 2020 pandemic, resulting from SARS-CoV 2, imposed the implementation of solutions responding to the needs emerged from confinement. In Portugal, within the scope of the proclaimed "state of emergency", measures were taken such as the decree of confinement, teleworking and the closure of educational institutions. These measures also had an impact on the activities developed in schools. This paper aims at describing the context and the need of promoting, in Portuguese schools, in a short period of time, the transition from face-to-face to a quick distance learning, which is different from a remote emergency teaching. The authors present part of a work in progress, embedded in a larger project, and describe the challenge posed to a multidisciplinary research team to devise short term courses at a distance based on the evidences brought to light from research on models of Distance Learning, aimed at teachers from non-higher education levels. With a Design-Based Research methodological approach the authors herein present one of the provisional results (Model 1) and some reflections about digital transformation in schools.

Keywords: COVID-19 Pandemic; Distance Learning; Remote Learning; Teachers' Training; MIREAD

Introduction

The COVID-19 disease caused by the SARS-CoV 2 virus was detected in December 2019. In January 2020, the World Health Organization declared the COVID-19 situation an International Public Health Emergency and, on March 11th 2020, it was considered a pandemic (WHO, 2020). Portugal tries to slow down the dissemination by decreeing emergency measures and subsequent confinement in the following days through law decree (DRE, 2020). These measures include, among others, teleworking and the closure of institutions and organizations, with the main purpose of promoting social distance and avoiding contagion. Education institutions, private and public, were included in these measures. The suspension of face-to-face school activities as a result of the enacted measures and the need to ensure the continuity of the 2019/2020 school year, leads to the Portuguese Government (PG) recommendation of implementing Distance Learning (DL) solutions for all educational institutions (DRE, 2020).

It matters, though briefly, to distinguish Distance Learning (DL) from Emergency Remote Teaching (ERT). In addition to the physical distance inherent to DL it also characterizes by careful instructional design and planning, covering content, communication, interaction, collaboration, activities and learning assessment. Also to be highlighted, is the role of the virtual learning environment (VLE) in the design of the teaching-learning process and the prevalence of asynchronous communication over synchronous, allowing high levels of space-time flexibility. As for the ERT, it characterizes by occurring in a punctual manner in emergency situations, seeking to provide a quick response and to fulfil the impossibility of face-to-face teaching. It involves a non-planned physical separation between teachers and students, and the contents, materials, activities and assessment are, roughly, transposed to a "at a distance scenario", privileging synchronous interaction and thus simulating presence classes/hours. In other words, the "affordances'' (Laurillard, 2002) of this ERT are the same that prevail in face-to-face teaching.

The COVID-19 subsequent lockdown, was perceived by the PG and by the educational stakeholders, as an exceptional situation, seeking to implement emergency solutions, with the purpose of ensuring the continuity of the school year in the most normalized way possible, providing "remote classes" (Bozkurt & Sharma, 2020). Portuguese schools were asked for rapid solutions as an attempt to overcome the suspension of face-to-face teaching, with the enormous need on the part of the schools to self-organize for the benefit of its students, however, "There was no revolution in the ways of teaching, but only in the means." (Alaiz, 2020; p.137)

Thus, we verify that we are neither facing DL nor other teaching modalities enriched by technologies, but rather "Remote Emergency Teaching" defined by some authors as "... a temporary shift of instructional delivery to an alternate delivery mode due to crisis circumstances" (Hodges et al., 2020). Hence, the emerging context brought to light previously existing gaps in the Portuguese society, both in terms of the access to equipment and internet or, at the level, of skills in its use, i.e. digital literacy. It was also evident that digital literacy of families, students and teachers remains below expectations, despite the implementation of European initiatives and at the national level, the IncoDE.2030 (Sá & Serpa, 2020). It is the general recognition of the unpreparedness of the majority of teachers and students, of the most varied teaching cycles, to implement DL solutions – that they did not know – leading to quality learning, that inspires the training proposal for teachers that we present on the following pages.

Distance learning in scholar education: Intensive and Rapid Teacher Training

It is in the pandemic and lockdown context that some schools recognize the existence of disparate levels within the technological infrastructure used at the schools (equipment and connectivity) and at home, both of teachers and students, the lack of digital resources in compliance with the curriculum, and at the level of digital skills of both teachers and students. Thus, schools developed a plan to support their educational environment, by distributing digital equipment and improving the connectivity quality, but also with regard to a rapid provision of training to the scholars, as well as requiring consultations through informal initiatives or professional groups and citizens.

This article presents part of a work in progress, integrated in a general project developed within the scope of the Investigation Unit (LE@D, UAb) that welcomes the authors. It describes the challenge posed to a multidisciplinary team of researchers to design short courses based on the research evidence of DL models and aimed for teachers and educators of schools (non-higher education) and applicable in different school scenarios.

Methodological Approach

The methodology used for developing intensive and rapid training proposals in distance learning is part of a design-based research (Anderson & Shatuck, 2012) that involved different phases of information collection:

1. focus group with a multidisciplinary team made up of teachers, psychologists, instructional designers, computer engineer, and school coordinators and directors;
2. in-depth interviews with key players from the educational institutions;
3. questionnaires answered by teachers and educators; and
4. design of differentiated scenarios of, intensive and rapid, DL.

In-between results

The attempted response to the problems felt by the schools led to a process of creating suitable solutions, which we now describe for only one of the scenarios: "Model 1 – Rapid Intervention in Distance Learning Model". With the urgency factor as a conditioning aspect, the developed Model 1: MIREAD is inspired by the "smart learning" trend and in a simplified learning design, in other words, is based on the development, implementation, awareness and effective start into practice in a very short period of time. MIREAD is structured around the aim to raise awareness of the real problem and potential solutions among the actors involved. The rapid implementation was triggered by the goal of continuing, in a sustained and balanced way, the ongoing work in the academic year 2019/2020. Due to the urgency of the situation and the profile of the actors involved in each institution, this model has components based on the characteristics of DL (Anderson & Dron, 2011), but introduces a component centred on synchronous communication and on the distribution of content one to many (Golden, 2020). Based on the collected data, it was possible to define some vectors of the model that we briefly describe:

- Actors' previous ideas: Based on the a priori collected information, the model foresees a deconstruction of preconceived ideas about DL and the use of technologies, which interfere in the action and change of behaviours to adopt throughout the training. For instance, preconceived ideas such as "distance education is a replica of classroom teaching", both in terms of communication and interaction and the role of the teacher (Quintas-Mendes et al., 2009) should be addressed;
- Access and familiarity with online technology and culture;
- Asynchronous versus synchronous communication: The type of communication to be used is one of the vectors that needs to be worked on, positioning this model as essentially based on asynchronous communication, which introduces flexibility in time and space, and which allows a diversified interaction between all the network actors. Synchronous moments must be consciously planned and designed to carry out concrete and time-bound activities (Wiederhold, 2020), which is well-grounded on research concerning immediacy in DL (Marquart et al., 2016);
- Physical to virtual space: It was possible to find out that actors are not familiar with the use of digital technologies and, in some cases, there are no infrastructures for the development of technology-mediated education. Therefore, special attention was given to this relationship, even because these aspects condition the communication and the pedagogical planning (Pimentel & Gomes, 2019).

The proposed model is based on two structuring elements of the teaching practice and student learning: the "Weekly Digital Learning Tool" (WDLT) and the "Virtual Learning Environment" (VLE).

The student's WDLT is an instrument created by the teacher. It presents the weekly planned work to be developed by the students and, at the same time, is an opportunity for dialogue between teachers and students and, of course, the families. It describes and specifies all the activities to be carried out, the final products to be created and which educational resources must be used, as well as the privileged communication channels to use, distributed by the various spaces and digital tools. It also structures the student's time required for the accomplishment of the proposed activities. In the case of students of lower age groups, the WDLT is also an instrument of communication with the scaffolding adult at home, who becomes a partner in its implementation.

The VLE (Pimentel & Gomes, 2019; Weller, 2020) combines an asynchronous communication environment, complemented by a synchronous one, in which the teacher and students act. This VLE has characteristics appropriate to different educational meanings and is organized by the teacher, taking into account the distinctiveness of the class, the curriculum and the students' age group. The technology used as VLE can be diverse, (Google Classroom, Moodle, etc.). It is in the VLE, in the space of each class/discipline, that the WDLT is made available to students, as well as the educational resources to be used, and where asynchronous communication takes place. The great advantage is that it allows the work to be carried out without meeting all at the same time and in the same space, depending on the student's temporal organization, maintaining one of the main characteristics of the DL models: flexibility. In this model, synchronous communication is weekly, promoted by the teacher and strongly delimited in time, with a duration of max. 20-40 minutes. The sessions must be planned in order to analyse the work done and corresponding to the WDLT. Regardless of the technology, the value of the synchronous session includes socio-emotional, collaboration and sharing aspects.

Good practice guide and recommendations

Teachers and students have to adapt to the emerging DL scenarios, developing new skills (digital, communicational) until they reach the necessary proficiency in this learning modality. When designing the WDLT, teachers should keep in mind that, in DL, concluding proposed tasks involves more time, greater autonomy, greater capacity for organization and individual time management, and a higher degree of self-motivation, than in face-to-face. Teachers must follow the accomplishment of activities proposed in the WDLT and monitor the communication in the asynchronous environment, answer questions, and give additional guidance. However, in this role of "online teacher" a balance must be found between professional overload and totally absent from the VLE. Thus, teachers must raise awareness of the efficient use of online communication channels available in the VLE, promoting the public posing and answering of questions in the class space.

Conclusion

Transition from traditional face-to-face systems to DL systems is a complex process, requiring technological infrastructures, human resources and the adoption of a specific pedagogy that is based on principles, characteristics and practices, resulting from research in DL. Recognizing that DL requires competences and characteristics far beyond the occasional ERT, this article focuses on lessons learned from the authors work in responding to training requests from schools in the lockdown scenario, that lead to the development of a model based mainly on asynchronous interaction, with some elements of synchronous interaction, to support the implementation of an effective and true DL model for a school community.

The following assumptions were made: distance teaching and learning should neither replicate nor simulate face-to-face models; it should preserve temporal and local flexibility, based on asynchronous communication; DL is based on teacher-student-content interaction. It was developed as a distance learning model which encompasses the conceptualization, implementation and monitoring of distance learning solutions. The proposed model foresees that the work with the students must be mainly asynchronous, based on weekly planned activities proposed by the teacher, with the support of the offered materials (educational resources in digital format). Thus, synchronous sessions should be limited to one per discipline, per week, lasting 20 to 40 minutes. Apart from supporting the rapid implementation of DL solutions, this training plan also aims to promote the development of teachers' skills in distance education, namely (a) pedagogical (emerging pedagogies); (b) social and communicational; (c) technological in context. Aware of the complexity and scope of the themes addressed in what concerns the e-professor's competences, it is intended in future investigations to assess the (non)acquisition of the mentioned skills by the trainees as well as the (non)adequacy of the model.

Regardless of the pandemic challenges facing us in 2020/21, there is a digital transformation underway that will have implications in all areas, namely in the area of education, in general, and also in the training of educational professionals: "In our rapidly changing world, education cannot rely on lessons of the past to prepare for the future. The future is here, and education systems need to learn from it. Our success will depend on how effectively we use our knowledge to anticipate the future, and how quickly we take action to shape it. " (OECD, 2020; p.8)

References

Alaiz, V. (2020). Impactos, metamorfoses, desigualdades e… expectativas. In J. M. Alves & I. Cabral (Eds.), *Ensinar e aprender em tempo de COVID 19: entre o caos e a redenção* (pp. 136-139). UCP.

Anderson, T., & Dron, J. (2011). Three generations of distance education pedagogy. *The International Review of Research in Open and Distance Learning, 12*(3), 80-97.

Anderson, T., & Shattuck, J. (2012). Design-Based Research: A Decade of Progress in Education Research? *Educational Researcher, 41*(1), 16-25. https://doi.org/10.3102/0013189X11428813

Bozkurt, A., & Sharma, R. (2020). Emergency remote teaching in a time of global crisis due to Corona Virus pandemic. *Asian Journal of Distance Education, 15*(1), 1-6.

DRE. (2020). *Several law decrets.* Retrieved from https://dre.pt/legislacao-covid-19-por-areas-tematicas

Golden, C. (2020). *Remote teaching: The glass half-full.* EDUCAUSE Review.

Hodges, C., Moore, S., Lockee, B., Trust, T., & Bond, A. (2020). The Difference between Emergency Remote Teaching and Online Learning. Educause Review, 27 march 2020.

Marquart, M., Fleming, M., Rosenthal, S. A., & Hibbert, M. (2016). Instructional Strategies for Synchronous Components of Online Courses. In D'Agustino, S. (Ed.), *Creating Teacher Immediacy in Online Learning Environments* (pp. 188-211). IGI Global.

Laurillard, D. (2002). *Rethinking university teaching: A conversational framework for the effective use of learning technologies.* Routledge/Falmer.

Pimentel, E. P., & Gomes, A. S. (2019). Ambientes Virtuais de Aprendizagem para uma Educação mediada por tecnologias digitais. In E. Santos, et al. (Eds.), *Informática na Educação*, Vol. 5. Porto Alegre: SBC.

Quintas-Mendes, A., Morgado, L., & Amante, L. (2008). Online Communication and E-Learning. In T. T. Kidd & H. Song (Eds.), *Handbook of Research on Instructional Systems and Technology: Vol. II.* ISR.

Sá, M. J., & Serpa, S. (2020). The Global Crisis Brought about by SARS-CoV-2 and Its Impacts on Education: An Overview of the Portuguese Panorama-ft. *Science Insights Education Frontiers, 5*(2), 525-530.

Weller, M. (2020). *25 Years of Ed Tech.* Athabasca University Press.

WHO. (2020). *Coronavirus disease (COVID-19) Pandemic.* World Health Organization.

"SUDDENLY WE WERE ALL ONLINE": PERCEPTIONS AND PRACTICES EXPERIENCED BY FACULTY AND STUDENTS DURING EMERGENCY TEACHING

Ana Paiva, Ana Runa, Carlos Seco, Elizabeth Mendes, Hugo Matos Pereira, João Paz, Lina Morgado, Márcia Vieira, Paula Cardoso, Laboratory of Distance Education & eLearning (LE@D), Portugal

ABSTRACT

This communication presents an ongoing research on the perceptions and practices experienced in Portuguese Higher Education Institutions, during the recent period of social confinement determined by the Portuguese Government, due to the COVID-19 pandemic. The main objective was to understand how Higher Education faculty and students experienced the digital transition to emergency education and the pedagogical practices adopted during that period. The research was based on a mixed methods approach. In order to address the research objectives and describe the pedagogical practices implemented, specific instruments were developed for data collection, namely: a questionnaire aimed at students and interviews aimed at both students and faculty. These cover technological and pedagogical dimensions, as well as the assessment of the experience.

The data collection took place at the end of the semester of the school year 2019-2020, with the participation of students and faculty from eight Higher Education Institutions (four Universities and four Polytechnic Institutes). The research results are currently under analysis.

Keywords: Distance Education, Emergency Remote Teaching, Online Pedagogical Practices.

Introduction

During the confinement period, Higher Education Institutions (HEIs) experienced new situations, due to the closure of physical spaces, and a huge disruption when transitioning from on-campus to online, on an unprecedented scale. In general, the institutional responses focused on a quick transition to emergency digital education, in what Zimmerman (2020) classified as the "Great Online-Learning Experiment", which demonstrated the resilience of the involved actors and educational organisations.

Although many Higher Education Institutions in Portugal have eLearning or distance learning offices or departments to support the use of educational technologies, their stages of development in this matter are different, as has been visible in the annual conferences of eLearning institutions and units held since 2011 – eLIES. In addition, Portugal had no specific distance learning legislation until 2019, when the first regulation in this field – DL 133/2019 – , was published.

In the context of COVID 19, all Higher Education Institutions made the move to "the online", by adopting emergency solutions to keep their programmes running. Thousands of students attended online classes; thousands of teachers taught their classes online. Worldwide, 1.5 billion students were affected (UNESCO, 2020; UNICEF, 2020). In this context, there were many initiatives by experts and HEIs, who created online communities of practice and diverse support networks, shared Open Educational Resources (OER), Open Educational Practices (OEP) and "on the spot courses" to provide formal and informal training. Support networks have also been created, for teachers and the academic community, in a way that no programme or political initiative for digital inclusion or funding for teachers' digital training has ever managed to accomplish (INCoDe.2030, or the forecasts of the Horizon Report, 2019).

Within this framework, it is important to outline what different authors define as "Emergency Remote Teaching" (ERT). According to Hodges, Moore, Lockee, Trust, and Bond (2020), ERT (…) "is a temporary shift of instructional delivery to an alternate delivery mode due to crisis circumstances. It involves the use of fully remote teaching solutions for instruction or education that would otherwise be delivered face-to-face or as blended or hybrid courses and that will return to that format once the crisis or emergency has abated. The primary objective in these circumstances is not to re-create a robust educational ecosystem but rather to provide temporary access to instruction and instructional supports in a manner that is quick to set up and is reliably available during an emergency or crisis". Murphy (2020) uses the term "emergency eLearning" instead.

This situation has brought the field of distance learning to the forefront, introducing inevitable comparisons. As Bozkurt and Sharrma refer (2020), the distinction between ERT and distance education is crucial, since it determines "(…) the degree to which educators believe in distance education these days will play a significant role in the prosperity of distance education in a post-COVID world" (p.2).

Furthermore, it is important to know the pedagogical strategies implemented, to understand whether their focus was predominantly on synchronous communication, thus replicating the pedagogy of the face-to-face classroom, creating a "zoom pedagogy or zoom university", with high levels of digital fatigue (Wiederhold, 2020), and high cognitive workload (Morris, 2020), for both faculty and students, added to a permanent effort of self-presentation (hyper-communication) (Walther, 1996; Anderson, 2003; Watts, 2019).

If some of the pedagogical practices developed tended to be teacher-centred, and not student-centred, as usual in distance learning (Bates, 2019), there was a need to look for practices that would contribute to focus the student's attention on the teaching-learning processes, coming closer to the student's central role in the educational process. Thus, the research aimed at understanding aspects of the students' experiences that are sometimes less valued in face-to-face classes, but are inseparable from the design of the significant and participated pedagogical scenarios involved. At the same time, it was important to research the often-widespread idea that the richness of emotional communication is poorer in online environments than in face-to-face environments (Quintas-Mendes et al., 2009), including the assumption that the richness of online emotional communication is linked to the adequacy of the strategies used (Derks, Fischer, & Bos, 2008; Paiva, Giger, Faísca, & Batista, 2011).

This exploratory research aims to identify students' perceptions about the academic experiences they lived during that period, to analyse how Higher Education faculty and students experienced the digital transition to emergency teaching and to identify the facilitating or hindering pedagogical strategies/practices developed, through the narratives of faculty and students.

Methodology

The current study is exploratory due to the contemporary nature and relevance of the theme, which focuses on the experience of rapid digital transition to an "emergency teaching", a scenario quite different from distance education. Through a mixed methods approach (Creswell & Clark, 2018: Hesse-Biber, 2010), data was collected through an online questionnaire applied to students and videoconference interviews (Salmons, 2012; Archibald et al., 2019) conducted with both faculty and students. The participants in this research are students and faculty from eight Portuguese Higher Education institutions, four from Universities (three public and one private) and four from Polytechnic Institutes (three public and one private), covering the regions of Lisbon and Tagus Valley, Alentejo and Algarve (Central and Southern Portugal). In total, 486 students answered the questionnaire and 40 interviews were conducted, 20 with faculty and 20 with students.

Instruments

The Questionnaire

The questionnaire, aimed at Higher Education students who experienced a transition to emergency teaching, was structured in order to get a narrative of the students' experiences, based on their perceptions of academic and personal experiences, during the period of emergency teaching.

This instrument was structured in five parts (consisting of 53 items), according to the objectives and corresponding dimensions defined for this first stage of the research. The following dimensions (with types and examples) were used:

- student profile (demographic, digital, distance education and online participation in academic activities), 10 closed and open questions (e.g., Q9: "What is your previous experience with distance education?");
- perceptions on communication and assessment practices: 6 closed questions with a Likert-type scale, from Never to Very Frequent (e.g., Q12: "During the emergency period, the online activities of the courses supported by the synchronous platform were ... motivating");
- perceptions on the practices of interaction with content, teacher and peers: 13 statements for students to position themselves on a Likert-type scale, from Never to Very Frequent (e.g., Q22: "The interaction between faculty/students in the course, during the emergency period, was similar to the one we had in face-to-face classes");
- perceptions on the processes of socio-cognitive and emotional adaptation, through a scale with 20 items, from 1-Totally Disagree to 5-Totally Agree (e.g., Q45: "I felt periods of stress in the days I was online for many hours").

The Interview

The interview was informed by the literature review on the subject, as well as the objectives and structuring questions of the research. For this purpose, semi-structured interview guides were developed (Flick, 2005; Fortin et al., 2009). These were organised around four themes, in order to guide the researcher during the interviews: (a) Interview participation consent; (b)

Personal and socio-economic data; (c) Previous experience with distance education and (d) Pedagogical practices experienced.

The faculty interview included six open questions, comprising the technological, pedagogical and assessment dimensions of the experience, with the following main objectives: (a) to outline the interviewee's personal profile (personal, socioeconomic and socio-professional data); (b) to know how familiar the interviewee was with online communication and distance education; (c) to identify the digital technologies / tools that were used during emergency remote teaching; (d) to understand the pedagogical design adopted during emergency remote teaching; (e) to understand how faculty assess their emergency remote teaching experience. In total, 20 interviews were conducted, with faculty from all participating institutions.

The student interview aimed at exploring in depth the information obtained through the previously applied questionnaire. The topics to be explored were identified in the analysis of closed responses and an exploratory content analysis of the responses to open questions. The aim was to identify results with little defined tendency or contradictory results, particularly in the responses to the open questions. As in the case of faculty, this interview was structured with open questions and similar objectives. The questions focused on the following topics: (a) previous experience with distance education; (b) technological conditions to follow classes; (c) adaptation to the emergency remote teaching process; (d) assessment of support and communication by/with faculty, interaction with colleagues, pedagogical methods implemented, assessment procedures and participation in classes; (e) suggestions to improve future online classes. The intention was to interview 10% of the students who had answered the questionnaire and volunteered for the interview, from each of the participating institutions.

All data collection instruments were previously validated, which allowed some items to be reformulated, some errors corrected and the average response time to be measured. The questionnaire was applied online, by the end of the second semester, between the end of May and July 2020. The collection of data from the students was requested to faculty and / or degree coordinators, who were informed about the research objectives and procedures. Data confidentiality was also guaranteed and their informed consent was requested.

The contacts for the interviews were made with faculty and students from Higher Education Institutions who were willing to collaborate in this exploratory research and where the questionnaires had been applied. The interviewees were initially invited to participate by telephone contact and later, the formal invitation was sent by email and the interview was scheduled to be conducted through the video-conferencing tool Zoom-Colibri or Skype. For ethical reasons, the participants were previously informed about the objectives and scope of the interview. Likewise, they were asked to consent to the video recording. The interviews were conducted individually, lasting between 20 and 30 minutes.

The statistical analysis of questionnaire data will be developed with the SPSS software, version 25. The content analysis of the interview data will be conducted with the MAXQDA 10 software.

Final Remarks

The data obtained with the questionnaire are currently under statistical analysis and interview data are in the stage of content analysis. However, a preliminary presentation can be made in advance during the conference. Through the narratives based on the perceptions of students and faculty, the current research intends to contribute for the discussion of good practices, focusing on understanding what can be improved and what can be avoided, in a scenario close to the academic year 2020/21, by reflecting on good reconstructed pedagogical practices in the post-pandemic transformation, accelerated by the digital experience.

References

Anderson, T. (2003). Getting the Mix Right Again: An Updated and Theoretical Rationale for Interaction. *The International Review of Research in Open and Distributed Learning, 4*(2).

Archibald, M. M., Ambagtsheer, R. C., Casey, M. G., & Lawless, M. (2019). Using Zoom Videoconferencing for Qualitative Data Collection: Perceptions and Experiences of Researchers and Participants. *International Journal of Qualitative Methods, 18*, 1-8.

Bozkurt, A., & Sharma, R. (2020). Emergency remote teaching in a time of global crisis due to Coronavirus pandemic. *Asian Journal of Distance Education, 15*(1), 1-6.

Bates, T. (2019). *Teaching in Digital Age.* Vancouver: Tony Bates Associates Ltd.

Creswell, J. W., & Clark, V. L. P. (2018). *Designing and conducting mixed methods research.* London: Sage. https://doi.org/10.1016/S0953-7562(10)80014-0

Derks, D., Fischer, A. H., & Bos, A. E. R. (2008). The role of emotion in computer-mediated communication: A review. *Computers in Human Behavior, 24*, 766-785.

EDUCAUSE. (2019). Horizon Report, 2019 Higher Education Edition.

Flick, U. (2005). *Métodos qualitativos na investigação científica.* Lisboa: Monitor.

Fortin, M.-F. E., Cotê, J., & Filion, F. (2009). *Fundamentos e etapas do processo de investigação.* Loures: Lusodidacta.

Hesse-Biber, S. N. (2010). *Mixed Methods Research. Merging theory with practice.* New York: The Guilford Press.

Hodges, C., Moore, S., Lockee, B., Trust, T., & Bond, A. (2020, March 27). The Difference between Emergency Remote Teaching and Online Learning. Educause Review [Blog post]. Retrieved from https://er.educause.edu/articles/2020/3/the-difference-between-emergency-remote-teaching-and-online-learning

Morgan, H. (2020). Best Practices for Implementing Remote Learning during a Pandemic. *Journal of Educational Strategies, Issues and Ideas, 93*(3), 134-140.

Morris, B. (2020, May 27). Why does Zoom exhaust you? Science has an answer. The Wall Street journal [Blog post]. Retrieved from https://www.wsj.com/articles/why-does-zoom-exhaust-you-science-has-an-answer-11590600269

Murphy, M. (2020). COVID-19 and emergency eLearning: Consequences of the securitization of higher education for post-pandemic pedagogy. *Contemporary Security Policy, 41*(3), 492-505.

Paiva, A., Giger, J.-C., Faísca, L., & Batista, L. (2011). Mais quente melhor': O impacto do papel informativo das emoções na CMC". *Revista Galego-Portuguesa de Psicoloxía e Educación, nº extra*, 371-382.

Quintas-Mendes, A., Morgado, L., & Amante, L. (2008). Online Communication and E-Learning. In T. T. Kidd & H. Song (Eds.), *Handbook of Research on Instructional Systems and Technology* (Vol. II.). Information Science Reference.

Salmons, J. (2012). *Cases in Online Interview Research.* London: SAGE Publications.

UNICEF. (2020). *UNICEF and Microsoft launch global learning platform to help address COVID-19 education crisis.* Retrieved from https://www.unicef.org/press-releases/unicef-and-microsoft-launch-global-learningplatform-help-address-covid-19-education

UNESCO. (2020). *COVID-19 education response.* Retrieved from https://en.unesco.org/covid19/educationresponse/globalcoalition

Walther, J. B. (1996). Computer-mediated communication: Impersonal, interpersonal, and hyperpersonal interaction. *Communication Research, 23*, 3-43.

Watts, L. (2019). Synchronous and Asynchronous communication in distance learning: a review of literature. *The Quarterly Review of Distance Education, 17*(1), 23-32.

Wiederhold, B. K. (2020). Connecting through Technology during the Coronavirus Disease 2019 Pandemic: Avoiding "zoom Fatigue. *Cyberpsychology, Behavior, and Social Networking, 23*(7), 437-438.

Zimmerman, J. (2020, March 10). Coronavirus and the Great Online-Learning Experiment. Chronicle of Higher Education [Blog post]. Retrieved from https://www.chronicle.com/article/coronavirus-and-the-great-online-learning-experiment/

ONLINE EXAMS AND THEIR FRAMEWORK

Christoph Jungbauer, Eszter Geresics-Földi, Ferdinand Porsche Fernfachhochschule, Austria

Abstract

Online exams are a necessity nowadays. But how can an online exam be designed in such a way that their knowledge can safely be checked? This analysis focuses on timing and metadata of online exams to gain information about possible collaboration within student groups.

Keywords: online exam, framework, metadata, open book, natural language processing

Introduction

"Siri, please take my online exam." "Okay". Thank God – at least the teachers say so – we are not yet ready for artificial intelligence to write our exams. But how can an online exam, in which the students are not present, be designed in such a way that their knowledge can be safely checked?

The goal is clear, students should acquire skills. To achieve this, knowledge must be transformed. In order to check the transfer, knowledge must be queried.

A controlling factor here is time, the more compact the duration of the examination is, the more likely people will fall back on existing knowledge. But what does it look like when Google is queried? Is it a competence to find things? Maybe to validate them? Is a collection of links to a question already a transfer of knowledge? Are there questions that you cannot simply google?

This thesis analyses online exams and their meta-data and log files to provide a first approach to secure design.

Methods

Setting

One way to prevent cheating is to design the IT environment so that the system is as secure as possible. This requires a lot of know-how (Heiser & McArthur, 2020; Lalitha & Periasamy, 2018; John et al., 2017).

Another approach is to transfer the concept of open book examinations in a lecture hall to the virtual learning environment (Green et al., 2016). In other words, people can have Google and other tools opened in the background, use books – whether online, e-book or classically printed – at any time. This corresponds to an everyday situation of research in an office environment. A controlling factor here is time, the more compact the duration of the examination is, the more likely people will fall back on existing knowledge. The main reasons to do online exams are flexibility, real life situations. The effort is almost the same as for a written test.

Basic Questions

- What do students do when taking online tests?
- Do they use other media in parallel?
- How do group work look like?
- How do they organize their time?
- What do we learn from them?

To conduct the survey, we analysed 4 exams at the FFH University of Applied Science.

Findings

Results in Figure 1 show, that time correlates positive to grading. Looking at the possible starting time, there is no difference regarding the result.

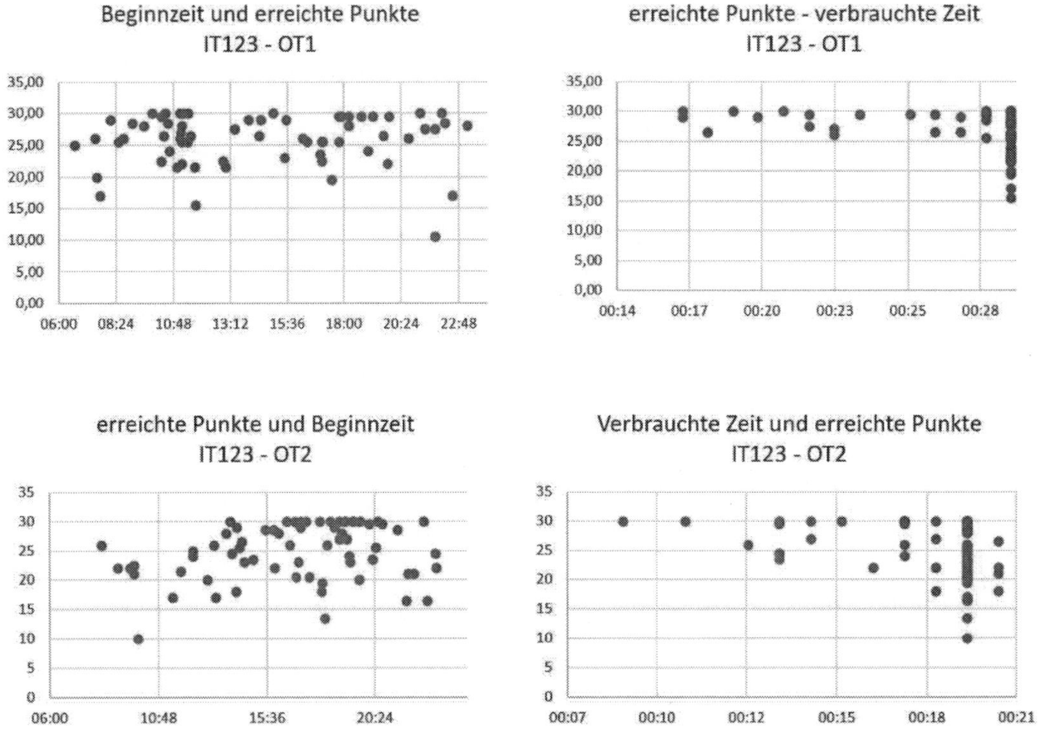

Figure 1. Measures from two exams

In a second step the metadata of the Moodle exams was examinated. Therefor we used Python with the GeoPandas package to do structure recognition and clustering. Figure 2 shows some of the metadata to uncover possible "offline" collaboration like students sitting at the same place.

Country Austria	**Region** Niederosterreich	**City** Maria Enzersdorf Report Incorrect Location	
ISP A1 Telekom Austria AG		**Coordinates of City** 48°6'0"N 16°16'60"E (48.1, 16.28333)	
Domain Name a1telekom.at	**Connection Type** DSL	**Usage Type** Fixed Line ISP, Mobile ISP	
Postcode 2344	**IDD Code** 43	**Area Code** 02236	**Elevation** 223 meters
Local Time 16 Feb, 2020 04:33 PM (UTC +01:00)		**Weather Station** Modling (AUXX0017) View Live Weather	

Figure 2. Detailed metadata of a student

Discussion

Analysis of the exams itself shows that time is a critical issue using open book exams in an online environment. If the time frame is too short, student will simply reproduce facts. If the time frame is too long the probability of collaboration will increase.

The analysis of the log data did not reveal useful aspects. Using the IP address to match a place is too inaccurate to correlate possible collaboration.

As a next step a third component – the language itself should be analysed using NLP (Natural Language Processing) techniques to check for authorship or group collaborations.

References

Green, S. G., Ferrante, C. J., & Heppard, K. A. (2016). Using Open-Book Exams to Enhance Student Learning, Performance, and Motivation. *Journal of Effective Teaching, 16*(1), 19-35.

Heiser, R. S., & McArthur, D. (2020). Online Accounting Education: How to Improve Security and Integrity of Students' Performance Assessments. *Journal of Instructional Pedagogies, 24*. Retrieved from https://eric.ed.gov/?id=EJ1263754

Lalitha, V., & Periasamy, J. K. (2018). Mobile based secured student online exam system. *International Journal of Engineering & Technology, 7*(1.7), 118-120. https://doi.org/10.14419/ijet.v7i1.7.9588

John, M. J., Ramakrishnan, S. H., Sirajudeen, M. A. M., & S., S. (2017). Advanced Online Examination using Raspberry Pi. *International Journal of Advanced Research Trends in Engineering and Technology (IJARTET), 4*, 345-349.